KIDS STUFF
ANGLiiSKi (English)

KIDS STUFF
ANGLiiSKi (English)

Лёгкие фразы на английском языке

(ESL)

(Easy English Phrases for Russian Speakers)

Therese Slevin Pirz

BILINGUAL KIDS SERIES

CHOU CHOU PRESS
P.O. BOX 152
SHOREHAM, N.Y. 11786
www.bilingualkids.com

Cataloging data: Pirz, Therese Slevin
                        Kids stuff angliiski (English): Easy English phrases for
                     Russian speakers.
                     Chou Chou Press, 2003
                        200 p. illus

                        Description: A collection of children's basic phrases
                     arranged by activity and rendered in English and Russian.
                     Pronunciation is given for the English sentences.

                        1. ESL – English as a second language 2. English language
                     3. Russian language 4. Russian phrases 5. English phrases
                     6. Russian conversation and phrase book 7. English conversation
                     and phrase book 8. Homeschooling
                     I. Title. II. Title: Easy English phrases for Russian speakers.
                     III. Series Bilingual Kids

Printed in the United States of America, 2003

First Edition.

ISBN   0-9716605-1-4

Order direct from the publisher:

                                        Chou Chou Press
                                        P.O. Box 152
                                        Shoreham, N.Y. 11786
                                        www.bilingualkids.com
                                        FAX: (631) 744-3423

May the Lord shed His
Light on us.

CONTENTS

Приветствие	GREETINGS	13
Ванная комната	THE BATHROOM	19
Одевание	GETTING DRESSED	24
Время еды	MEALTIME	27
Разговор	CONVERSATION	34
Помощь по дому	HELPING at HOME	63
Уроки в доме	SCHOOL at HOME	70
Похвала	PRAISE	78
Покупки	SHOPPING	82
Весело!	FUN !	90
В субботу днём	SATURDAY AFTERNOON	110
Восклицания	EXCLAMATIONS	121
Празднование дня рождения	BIRTHDAY PARTY	132
Пора спать	BEDTIME	136
Погода	WEATHER	144
Время	TIME	148
Количество	QUANTITIES	151
Алфавит	ALPHABET	156
Детские песенки	NURSERY RHYMES	158
Молитвы	PRAYERS	163

Словарь/VOCABULARY

Семья, Ласковые слова,	165	Family, Endearments,
Цвета, Дни	165	Colors, Days
Месяца, Времена, Праздники,	166	Months, Time, Holidays,
Детская комната	166	Nursery
Игрушки	167	Toys
Одежда	168	Clothing
Развлечения, Тело человека	169	Entertainments, Body
Напитки, Ёмкости, Десерт	170	Drinks, Containers, Dessert
Овощи, Мясные блюда, Рыбные блюда	171	Vegetables, Meat, Fish
Фрукты, Другие продукты	172	Fruit, Other Foods
Кухонные принадлежности, Дом,	173	Utensils, House
Жилище	173	Dwellings
Кухня, Ванная комната	174	Kitchen, Bathroom
Спальня, Гостиная, Инструменты	175	Bedroom, Living Room, Tools
Машина, Магазины, Профессии	176	Car, Stores, Occupations
Насекомые	177	Insects
Деревья, Животные	178	Trees, Animals
Птицы, Цветы	179	Birds, Flowers
Вдоль дороги	180	Along the Road

Руководство по произошению – PRONUNCIATION GUIDE 181
Индекс   – INDEX   185

Child's name:_____

Received this book from:_____

Occasion:_____Date:_____

First indication of child's understanding English:_____

_____

Child's first English word:_____

Child's favorite English word:_____

Favorite English books or stories:_____

_____

_____

Favorite American songs:_____

_____

Favorite American movies or videos:_____

_____

_____

Favorite things to do in English:_____

_____

_____

_____

Favorite American foods:_____

_____

PREFACE

The purpose of <u>Kids Stuff Angliiski</u> is to enable speakers of Russian to learn English (ESL – English as a Second Language) in a practical, personal and easy manner, and at the same time to teach their children as well.

The term "kids stuff" implies something extremely simple and easy. That is how we anticipate users finding the sentences and pronunciations in this book. The over one thousand sentences are merely the basic framework on which to build many more sentences and expressions. The amount of those sentences is limitless.

The ease of using <u>Kids Stuff Angliiski</u> enables the user to start speaking English without looking up meanings, pronunciation, grammar and vocabulary in order to express simple ideas about every day experiences.

<u>Kids Stuff Angliiski</u> is for adults, parents, children, students, teachers and travelers --- all those who wish to speak English correctly in a short time.

Good luck learning English the <u>Kids Stuff</u> way. Knowledge of English will open many new doors of opportunity.

В ГОСТЯХ ХОРОШО, А ДОМА ЛУЧШЕ

Приветствие   Gr<u>ee</u>tings

Start your day and your conversations here. Saying the first few words in English will help you build momentum to continue speaking English for the rest of the day. Hearing and speaking English will make you feel cheerful especially when it is spoken by you or to you by your little one.

Здравствуйте!	Hello! *HEL-oh!* (or) *Hel-OH!*
Алло!	Hello! (Answering the telephone)
Слушаю. Кто у телефона?	Hello. Who's speaking? (Answering the telephone.) *HEL-oh!* (or) *Hel-OH!* *Hooz SPEEK-'ng?*

Приветствие _____

Это я! Это........ говорит.

Speaking! This is...speaking.
SPEE-k'ng! This iz...SPEEK-'ng.

Это я!

It is I. (Polite) It's me. (Slang)
It iz igh. Itz mee.

√ Я тебе перезвоню.

I'll call you back.
Ighl kawl yoo bak.

Позвони....

Call...
Kawl...

До свидания.

Goodbye.
Gud-BIGH.

Всего хорошего!

All the best!
Awl th'best!

Доброе утро.

Good morning.
Gud MORN-'ng.

Добрый день.

Good day. Hi!
Gud dei. High!

Добрый вечер.

Good evening.
Gud EEV-ning.

Спокойной ночи.

Good night.
Gud night.

До завтра!

Until tomorrow!
Uhn-TIL tuh-MAHR-oh!

Войди! (после стука в дверь)

Come in! (after knocking)
Kuhm in! (AF-ter NAHK-'ng)

Рад/ Рада/ тебя видеть.

I'm glad to see you.
Ighm glad t'see yoo.

Я рад/-а тебе.

It's good to see you.
Itz gud t'see yoo.

Как дела?

How goes it! How are things?
Haou gohz it? Haou ahr th'ngz?

Как поживаешь?

How are you?
Haou ahr yoo?

Как ты себя чувствуешь?

How do you feel?
Haou doo yoo feel?

Выздоравливай.

Get well soon.
Get wel soon.

У меня всё.

I'm all right.
Ighm awl right.

(Очень) хорошо спасибо.

(Very) well, thanks.
(VER-ee) wel, thanks.

Что нового?

What's new?
Wahtz noo?

(У меня) ничего нового!

Nothing new (with me)!
NUHTH-'ng noo (with mee)!

Я буду скучать без тебя.

I will miss you.
Igh wil mis yoo.

Скучал/-а ли ты без меня?

Did you miss me?
Did yoo mis mee?

Что ты мне привёз/
привезла/?

What did you bring me?
Waht did yoo bring me?

Обними меня.

Give me a hug.
Giv mee uh huhg.

Приветствие

Поцелуй меня!	Give me a kiss! *Giv mee uh kis!*
Что я могу сделать для тебя?	What can I do for you? *Waht kan igh doo for yoo?*
Помочь тебе?	Do you need any help? *Doo yoo need EN-ee help?*
Мне плохо. Не хорошо.	Not so good. Not so well. *Naht soh gud. Naht soh wel.*
Так себе.	So so. *Soh soh.*
До скорого. Пока.	See you later. So long. *See yoo LEI-tr. Soh lawng.*
До скорого! До свидания.	See you soon! Goodbye. *See yoo soon! Gud-BIGH.*
Желаю хорошо провести время!	Have a good time! *Hav uh gud tighm!*
Счастливого пути!	Have a good trip! *Hav uh gud trip!*
Передай привет	Say hello to... *Sei hel-OH too...*
Помаши рукой.	Wave good-bye. *Weiv gud-BIGH.*
Извини.	Excuse me. *Ek-SKYOOZ mee.*
Прости!	I beg your pardon! *Igh beg yor PAHR-duhn!*

Всего доброго! (or) Желаю успеха!	Good luck! *Gud luhk!*
Слава Богу!	Thank God! *Thank Gahd!*
Благослови тебя Бог!	God bless you! *Gahd bles yoo!*
Поздравляю!	Congratulations! *Kuhn-grad-jyuh-LEI-shuhnz!*
С днем рождения!	Happy Birthday! *HAP-ee BIRTH-dei!*
С рождеством Христовым!	Merry Christmas! *MEHR-ee KRIS-muhs!*
С Новым Годом!	Happy New Year! *HAP-ee Noo Yeer!*
Будь здоров/-а!	Bless you! *Bles yoo!*
Твоё здоровье!	To your health! *Too yor helth!*
Пожалуйста.	Please. *Pleez.*
(Нет) Спасибо. Большое спасибо.	(No), thank you. Thanks a lot. *(Noh), thank yoo. Thanks uh laht.*
Спасибо за всё, что ты для меня сделал/-а.	Thank you for all you have done. *Thank yoo for awl yoo hav duhn.*

Приветствие _____

Пожалуйста. (or) Не́ за что.	You're welcome. *Yor WEL-kuhm.*
Добро пожаловать!	Welcome! *WEL-kuhm!*
Очень/ рад/ рада/ с тобой познакомиться.	I'm glad to meet you. *Ighm glad t'meet yoo.*
Ты говоришь по-английски?	Do you speak English? *Doo yoo speek ING-lish?*
Как сказать...?	How do you say....? *Haou doo yoo sei...?*
Я (не) говорю по-английски.	I (don't) speak English. *Igh (dohnt) speek ING-lish.*
Как тебя зовут?	What is your name? *Waht iz yor neim?*
Меня зовут...	My name is ... *Migh neim iz...*
Где ты живёшь?	Where do you live? *Wehr doo yoo liv?*
Добрый день!	Have a nice day! *Hav uh nighs dei!*

we must, we must wash up. From morning until night.

Нада, нада умываться, По утрам и вечерам.*

Ванная комната   ## The Bathroom

Every family member knows how much time is spent in the bathroom showering, bathing, singing, soaking, admiring.... A good time to practice your English looking in the mirror or aloud in the shower.

Сходи в туалет.

Go to the bathroom. (toilet)
Goh t'th'BATH-room. (TOY-let)

У тебя грязное лицо. Вымой его.

Your face is dirty. Wash it.
Yor feis iz DIRT-ee. Wahsh it.

Помой/ руки/ уши/.

Wash your/ hands/ ears/.
Wahsh yor/ hanz/ eerz/.

Умойся.

Wash your face.
Wahsh yor feis.

19

Ванная комната _____

/Скажи мне/ Ты мне сказал-а/
когда тебе нужно...

Tell me/ You told me/ when
you have...
*Tel mee/ Yoo tohld mee/ wen
yoo hav...*

...сходить в туалет.

...to go to the toilet.
...t'goh t'th'TOY-let.

Спусти за собой (воду).

Flush the toilet.
Fluhsh th'TOY-let.

Закрой туалетную крышку.

Put down the seat.
Put daoun th'seet.

Давай помоем руки.

Let's wash up.
Letz wahsh ahp.

Не забудь помыть руки.
(перед едой/ ужином)

Don't forget to wash your
hands. (before a meal or
dinner)
*Dohnt for-GET t'wahsh yor
hanz. (bee-FOR uh meel or
DIN-er)*

Ты помыл/-а шею?

Did you wash your neck?
Did yoo wahsh yor nek?

Почисти зубы после еды.

Brush your teeth after eating.
*Bruhsh yor teeth AF-ter
EET-'ng.*

Прочисти ниткой между зубами.

Floss between your teeth.
Flaws bee-TWEEN yor teeth.

Твоя зубная щётка на раковине.

Your toothbrush is on the sink.
*Yor TOOTH-bruhsh iz awn
th'sink.*

Помни, что надо почистить зубы.

Remember to brush your teeth.
Ree-MEM-ber t'bruhsh yor teeth.

Ты не вымыл/-а лицо.

You didn't wash your face.
Yoo DID'nt wahsh yor feis.

Ты/ весь/ вся/ чистый/-ая?

Are you all clean?
Ahr yoo awl kleen?

Ты выгладишь чистым.

You look clean.
Yoo luk kleen.

У тебя чистые лицо и руки.

Your face and hands are clean.
Yor feis and hanz ahr kleen.

Тебе нужно принять ванну.

You need to take a bath.
Yoo need t'teik uh bath.

/Открой/ Закрой/ кран.

Turn the faucet/ on/ off/.
Tern th'FAW-set/ ahn/ awf/.

Ты принимаешь ванну ?

Are you taking a bath?
Ahr yoo TEIK-'ng uh bath?

Я готовлю для тебя ванну.

I'm running a bath for you.
Ighm RUHN-'ng uh bath for yoo.

Видишь, как течёт вода ?

See the water run?
See th'WAW-ter ruhn?

Вода слишком/ горячая/
холодная/.

The water is too/ hot/ cold/.
*Th'WAW-ter iz too/ haht/
kohld/.*

Не наливай в ванну слишком
много воды.

Don't fill the tub with too
much water.
*Dohnt fil th'tuhb with too
muhch WAW-ter.*

Я мою твою спину, колени и
животик.

I'm washing your back,
knees and tummy.
*Ighm WAHSH-'ng yor bak,
neez and TUHM-mee.*

21

Ванная комната

Как ты брызгаешь!

How you splash!
Haou yoo splash!

Помойся с мылом.

Use soap.
Yooz sohp.

Мыло хорошо пахнет,
но оно скользкое.

The soap smells good,
but it is slippery.
*Th'sohp smelz gud,
buht it iz SLIP-ree.*

Не так много:

мыла, воды,
зубной пасты,
дезодоранта.

Not so much:
Naht soh muhch:
soap *(sohp)*, water (*WAW-ter)*,
toothpaste (*TOOTH-peist)*,
deodorant (*dee-OH-d'r-ent*) .

Как следует вытрись, прежде
чем выйти из ванной.

Dry yourself well before
leaving the bathroom.
*Drigh yor-SELF wel bee-FOR
LEEV-'ng th'BATH-room.*

Спусти воду.

Empty the tub.
EMP-tee th'tuhb.

Вычисти (or Вымой) ванну.

Clean the tub.
Kleen th'tuhb.

Сложи полотенце.

Fold the towel.
Fohld th'taoul.

Положи полотенце в стирку.

Put the towel in the laundry.
Put th'taoul in th'LAWN-dree.

Повесь полотенце.

Hang up the towel.
Hang ahp th'taoul.

Ты выключил/-а свет?

Did you turn out the light?
Did yoo tern aout th'light?

Ты хотел/-а бы принять ванну?	Would you like to take a bath? *Wud yoo lighk t'teik uh bath?*
Нет. Я не хочу (принимать ванну).	No. I don't want to (take a bath). *Noh. Igh dohnt wahnt too (teik uh bath).*
Тебе нужно/ постричься/ побриться/.	You need/ a haircut/ to shave/. *Yoo need / uh HEHR-kuht/ t'sheiv/.*
Потом помой голову!	Wash your hair later! *Wahsh yor hehr LEIT-er!*
Ты хорошо выглядишь.	You look good. *Yoo luk gud.*

* from page 19 "Мойдодыр" by Tchukovsky

Leave well enough alone.

От добра добра не ищут

Одевание   Getting Dressed

Is it to be the cowboy outfit or the space suit this morning? When you are in a hurry these are not options. Perhaps, instead, when your little girl dresses her dolls, or your little guy is playing with his action figures, you and they can try some of these phrases.

Вставай! Уже пора вставать!

Get up! It's time to get up!
Get ahp! Itz tighm t'get ahp!

Я меняю твой подгузник.

I'm changing your diaper.
Ighm *CHEINJ- 'ng yor DIGH-pr.*

Просунь руку в рукав.

Put your hand through the sleeve.
Put yor hand throo th'sleev.

Я надеваю правую туфлю.

I'm putting on your right shoe.
Ighm PUT- 'ng ahn yor right shoo.

24

На тебе не тот ботинок.

You have the wrong shoe on.
Yoo hav th'rawng shoo ahn.

Застегни рубашку.

Button your shirt.
BUHT-uhn yor shert.

Я не могу решить, что надеть.

I can't decide what to wear.
Igh kant d'SIGHD waht t' wehr.

Ты хочешь надеть белую или синюю блузку?

Do you want to wear the white or the blue blouse?
Doo yoo wahnt t'wehr th' wight or th'bloo blaous?

Где твоя шляпа?

Where is your hat?
Wehr iz yor hat?

Застегни молнию на куртке.

Close the zipper on your jacket.
Klohz th'ZIP-er ahn yor JAK-et.

Ищи свои перчатки.

Look for your gloves.
Luk for yor gluhvz.

Папа пошёл на работу.

Daddy has gone to work.
DAD-ee haz gahn t'werk.

Пора одеваться.

It's time to get dressed.
Itz tighm t'get drest.

Нам нужно одеваться.

We have to get dressed.
Wee hav t'get drest.

Перестань кусать ногти!

Stop biting your nails!
Stahp BIGHT-'ng yor neilz!

Надень нижнее бельё и брюки.

Put on your underpants and pants.
Put ahn yor UHN-der-pantz and pantz.

25

Одевание_____

Надень новое пальто.

Wear your new coat.
Wehr yor noo koht.

Причешись.

Comb or brush your hair.
Kohm or bruhsh yor hehr.

Давай я тебя подстригу.

Let me trim your hair.
Let mee trim yor hehr.

Щётка и расчёска на туалетном столе.

The brush and comb are on the dresser.
Th'bruhsh and kohm ahr ahn th'DRES-er.

(Хоть) переоденься.

(At least) change your clothes.
(*At leest) cheinj yor klohz.*

Можешь надеть футболку.

The T-shirt will be fine.
Th'TEE-shert wil bee fighn.

Как ты хорошо выглядишь!

How nice you look!
Haou nighs yoo luk!

Everyone to his own taste.

Как начей вкус

Время еды

Meal Time

"Beverages," "Desserts," and "Meats," pages in this book will help expand your food vocabulary. You can even pretend you and your children are a bird from the "Birds" page. Select the "Insects" birds find appetizing. (Something to do AFTER eating!)

Давайте кушать! Перестань играть.	Let's eat! Stop playing. *Letz eet! Stahp PLEI-'ng.*
Сейчас же ешь!	Eat now! *Eet naou!*
Тебе хочется позавтракать?	Do you feel like eating breakfast? *Doo yoo feel lighk EET-'ng BREK-fest?*

27

Время еды_____

Сейчас я не хочу.	I don't want to now. *Igh dohnt wahnt too naou.*
Иди за стол, пожалуйста.	Come to the table, please. *Kuhm t'th'TEI-bl, pleez.*
Когда мы будем обедать?	When are we having lunch? *Wen ahr wee HAV-'ng luhnch?*
Ты/ голоден/ голодна/?	Are you hungry? *Ahr yoo HUHNG-ree?*
Я (так)/ голоден/ голодна/.	I'm (so) hungry.· *Ighm (soh) HUHNG-ree.*
Я умираю с голоду!	I'm starving! *Ighm STAHRV-'ng!*
Мне хочется пить.	I'm thirsty. *Ighm THER-stee.*
Что бы ты хотел/-а поесть?	What would you like to eat? *Waht wud yoo lighk t'eet?*
Ты хотел/ хотела/ бы что-нибудь поесть?	Would you like something to eat? *Wud yoo lighk SUHM-th'ng t'eet?*
Я возьму...	I'll have... *Ighl hav...*
Как на счёт ужина?	What about dinner? *Waht uh-BAOUT DIN-er?*
Что у нас на ужин?	What do we have for dinner? *Waht doo wee hav for DIN-er?*
Что ты делал/-а сегодня?	What did you do today? *Waht did yoo doo tuh-DEI?*

Ты ничего не ел/-а.

You have not eaten anything.
*Yoo hav naht EET-'n
EN-ee-th'ng.*

Когда мы будем кушать?

When are we eating?
Wen ahr wee EET-'ng?

Кто хочет кушать?

Who wants to eat?
Hoo wahntz t'eet?

Ужин готов.

Dinner is ready.
DIN-er iz RED-ee.

Давайте сядем (за стол).

Let's sit down.
Letz sit daoun.

Сядь рядом/ со мной/ с ним/
с ней/.

Sit near/ me/ him/ her/.
Sit neer/ mee/ him/ her/.

Сядь (правильно).

Sit down (correctly).
Sit daoun (kuh-REKT-lee).

Убери локти со стола.

Take your elbows off the table.
Teik yor EL-bohz awf th'TEI-bl.

Давай перекусим.

Let's have a snack.
Letz hav uh snak.

Разогрей пиццу в микроволновке.

Warm the pizza in the micro.
*Wahrm th'PEETZ-uh in
th'MIGH-kroh.*

Ты хочешь бекон или картофель?

Do you want bacon or potatoes?
*Doo yoo wahnt BEI-kuhn or
poh-TEI-tohz?*

Возьми, пожалуйста.

Help yourself.
Help yor-SELF.

Время еды

Возьми ещё немного.	Take some more.
	Teik suhm mor.
Сделай себе сандвич.	Make yourself a sandwich.
	Meik yor-SELF uh SAN-wich.
Можно мне ещё морковки?	May I have more carrots?
	Mei igh hav mor KAR-uhtz?
Хочешь добавки ?	Do you want another helping?
	Doo yoo wahnt uh-NUTH-er
	HELP-'ng?
А мне что-нибудь осталось?	Is there any more left for me?
	Iz thehr EN-ee mor left for mee?
Поделись печеньем.	Share your cookie.
	Shehr yor KUK-ee.
Я бы съел ещё немного каши.	I'll take a little more cereal.
	Ighl teik uh LIT-ul mor SEER-ee-ul.
Хочу ещё порцию каши.	I want another helping of cereal.
	Igh wahnt uh-NUTH-er HELP-'ng
	uhv SEER-ee-ul.
Мне достаточно.	I am still hungry.
	Igh am stil HUHNG-ree.
Я больше не хочу. Я сыт.	I don't want any more. I'm full.
	Igh dohnt wahnt EN-ee mor. Ighm ful.
Можно попробовать немного?	May I have a taste?
	Mei Igh hav uh teist?
Да, чуть-чуть.	Yes, a little.
	Yes, uh LIT-ul.
Я тоже хочу.	I want some too.
	Igh wahnt suhm too.

Что ты пьёшь?	What are you drinking? *Waht ahr yoo DRINK-'ng?*
Что ты/ пил/ пила/?	What did you drink? *Waht did yoo drink?*
Я больше не могу есть.	I cannot eat any more. *Igh KAN-naht eet EN-ee mor.*
Есть больше нечего.	There is no more. *Thehr iz noh mor.*
Передай, пожалуйста, соль?	Would you pass the salt? *Wud yoo pas th'sawlt?*
Пользуйся вилкой, ножом, ложкой.	Use your fork, knife, spoon. *Yooz yor fork, nighf, spoon.*
Не жми банан в руке.	Don't squeeze the banana in your hand. *Dohnt skweez th'buh-NAN-uh in yor hand.*
Осторожно, не проглоти косточку.	Be careful not to swallow the pit. *Bee KEHR-ful naht t'SWAHL-oh 'th'pit.*
Давай я порежу тебе мясо.	Let me cut your meat. *Let mee kuht yor meet.*
Не пей так быстро молоко!	Don't drink your milk so fast! *Dohnt drink yor milk soh fast!*
Накрывай бутылку.	Put the cover on the bottle. *Put th'KUHV-er ahn th'BAHT-le.*
Съешь немного. Пробуй это.	Eat (just) a little. Try it. *Eet (juhst) uh LIT-ul. Trigh it.*
Еда хорошо пахнет.	The food smells good. *Th'food smelz gud.*

31

Время еды

Это вкусно? Мне нравится.	Is it tasty ? I like it. *Iz it TEIST-ee? Igh lighk it.*
Пудинг/ сладкий/ солёный/.	The pudding is/ sweet/ salty/. *Th'PUD-'ng iz/ sweet/ SAWLT-ee/.*
Соус очень/ горький/ кислый/ острый/.	The sauce is/ bitter/ sour/ spicy/. *Th'saws iz/ BIT-er/ SAOU-er/ SPIGHS-ee/.*
Можно мне глоточек?	Can I have a sip? *Kan igh hav uh sip?*
Ешь шпинат.	Eat your spinach. *Eet yor SPIN-ich.*
Мне нравятся бобы.	I like green beans. *Igh lighk green beenz.*
Ты можешь есть/ сам/ сама/.	You can feed yourself. *Yoo kan feed yor-SELF.*
Не говори с полным ртом.	Don't speak with your mouth fuJl. *Dohnt speek with yor maouth ful.*
Налей молоко в стакан.	Pour the milk in the glass. *Por th'milk in th'glas.*
Режь хлеб осторожно.	Cut the bread carefully. *Kuht th'bred KEHR-ful-ee.*
Не наливай в стакан воды.	Don't fill the glass with water. *Dohnt fil th'glas with WAW-ter.*
Стакан полон.	The glass is full. *Th'glas iz ful.*
Ты пролил/-а молоко.	You spilt some milk. *Yoo spilt suhm milk.*

Почему ты так много ешь?	Why do you eat so much? *Wigh doo yoo eet soh muhch?*
Доешь ужин.	Finish your dinner. *FIN-ish yor DIN-er.*
Допей/ молоко/ апельсиновый сок/.	Finish your /milk/ orange juice/. *FIN-ish yor/ milk/ OR-einj jyoos/.*
ты доел/-а?	Have you finished eating? *Hav yoo FIN-isht EET-'ng?*
Ты/ съел/ съела/ всё, что было на тарелке.	You have eaten everything on your plate. *Yoo hav EET-en EV-ree-th'ng ahn yor pleit.*
Можешь поиграть после ужина.	You can play after dinner. *Yoo kan plei AF-ter DIN-er.*
Приятного аппетита!	Enjoy your meal! *En-JOY yor meel!*
(Всё) было вкусно! Очень вкусно!	That (Everything) was delicious! *That (EV-ree-th'ng) wuhz dee-LISH-uhs!*
/Обед/ Ужин/ был очень вкусный.	/Lunch/ Dinner/ was delicious. */Luhnch/ DIN-er/ wuhz dee-LISH-uhs.*
Всё!	All gone! *Awl gahn!*
Можно мне выйти из-за стола?	May I leave the table? *Mei igh leev th'TEI-bl?*

A friend in need is a friend indeed.

Друзья познаются в беде

Разговор	Conversation

These are the pages you use to enlist, explain, persuade, coax, and insist when speaking with your child. When all else fails, there is always, Потому что я так сказал/-а. ("Because I say so!") – appropriate justification in any language.

Что это? Какой шум!

What is that? What a noise!
Waht iz that? Waht uh noiz!

Что ты слышишь?

What do you hear?
Waht doo yoo heer?

Я тебя напугал/-а?

Did I frighten you?
Did igh FRIGHT- 'n yoo?

Могу я чем-нибудь помочь?

Is there anything I can do?
Iz thehr EN-ee-th'ng igh kan doo?

Что ты говоришь?

What are you saying?
Waht ahr yoo SEI- 'ng?

Думай, прежде чем говоришь.	Think before you speak. *Think bee-FOR yoo speek.*
Что ты сказал/-а?	What did you say? *Waht did yoo sei?*
Я слушаю.	I'm listening. *Ighm LIS-'ng.*
Как ты красиво поёшь!	How beautifully you sing! *Haou BYOO-tif-lee yoo sing!*
Какой/ая ты разговорчивый/-ая!	How talkative you are! *Haou TAWK-uh-tiv yoo ahr!*
Ну-ка сиди прямо. (Command)	Come on! Sit up straight. *Kuhm ahn! Sit ahp streit.*
Сядь ко мне на колени. (Invitation)	Sit on my lap. *Sit ahn migh lap.*
Подними голову.	Raise your head. *Reiz yor hed.*
Возьми. Не бери...	Take it. Don't take... *Teik it. Dohnt teik ...*
Где погремушка?	Where is the rattle? *Wehr iz th'RAT-le?*
/Держи/ Возьми/ погремушку.	/Hold/ Take/ the rattle. */Hohld/ Teik/ th'RAT-le.*
Отпусти (меня)!	Let (me) go! *Let (mee) goh!*
На что ты смотришь?	What are you looking at? *Waht ahr yoo LUK-'ng at?*

35

Разговор

Я ищу...

I'm looking for...
Ighm LUK- 'ng for...

О чём ты думаешь?

What are you thinking about?
Waht ahr yoo THINK- 'ng uh-BAOUT?

Чему ты улыбаешься?

What are you smiling at?
Waht ahr yoo SMIGHL- 'ng at?

Я вижу, что ты мечтаешь.

I can see you're dreaming.
Igh kan see yor DREEM- 'ng.

Покажи мне, как ты двигаешь руками!

Show me how you move your arms!
Shoh mee haou yoo moov yor ahrmz!

Кто/ я/ он/ она/ это/?

Who/ am I/ is he/ is she/is it/?
Hoo/ am igh/ iz hee/ iz shee/ iz it/?

Я тебя знаю.

I know you.
Igh noh yoo.

Это/ твой брат/ твоя сестра/.

It's your/ brother/ sister/.
Itz yor/ BRUTH-er/ SIS-ter/.

Он/ маленький/ большой/.

He is/ small/ large/.
Hee iz/ smawl/ lahrj/.

Она/ маленькая/ большая/.

She is/ small/ large/.
Shee iz/ smawl/ lahrj/.

Оно/ маленькое/ большое/.

It is/ small/ large/.
It iz/ smawl/ lahrj/.

У тебя глаза совсем как у твоего отца.

You have eyes just like your father's.
Yoo hav ighz juhst lighk yor FAHTH-erz.

Улыбнись, пожалуйста!

Please, smile!
Pleez, smighl!

Я хочу тебя сфотографировать.

I want to take your picture.
Igh wahnt t'teik yor PIK-chur.

Сделай приятную улыбку!

Show me a nice smile!
Shoh mee uh nighs smighl!

Какой длинный рассказ!

What a long story!
Waht uh lawng STOR-ee!

Тебе нравится, не правда ли!

You like that, don't you!
Yoo lighk that, dohnt yoo!

Давай я потру тебе животик.

Let me rub your tummy.
Let mee ruhb yor TUM-ee.

Куда ты идёшь?

Where are you going?
Wehr ahr yoo GOH-'ng?

Посмотри на...

Look at.....
Luk at...

Ты видишь...?

Do you see...?
Doo yoo see...?

Повернись кругом.

Turn around.
Tern uh-ROUND.

Ты можешь держать мышь?

Can you hold the mouse?
Kan yoo hohld th'maous?

Что у тебя во рту?

What do you have in your mouth?
Waht doo yoo hav in yor maouth?

Тебе нельзя это брать в рот.

You cannot put that in your mouth.
Yoo KAN-naht put that in yor maouth.

37

Разговор

Не/ ударяй/ плескайся/ кусайся/ плачь/!	No/ kicking/ splashing/ biting/ crying/! *Noh/ KIK-'ng/ SPLASH-'ng/ BIGHT-'ng/ KRIGH-'ng/!*
Не ударяй меня ногой!	Don't kick me! *Dohnt kik mee!*
Как ты ударяешь ногой!	How you kick! *Haou yoo kik!*
Ты мочишь меня водой!	You're getting me wet! *Yor GET-'ng mee wet!*
Не плачь. Почему ты плачешь?	Don't cry. Why are you crying? *Dohnt krigh. Wigh ahr yoo KRIGH-'ng?*
Я плачу, потому что...	I'm crying because... *Ighm KRIGH-'ng bee-KAWZ...*
Я слышал/-а, как ты плачешь.	I heard you crying. *Igh herd yoo KRIGH-'ng.*
Где кубики?	Where are the blocks? *Wehr ahr th'blahks?*
Достань кубик.	Reach for the block. *Reech for th'blahk.*
Хочешь поиграть в мяч?	Would you like to play with the ball? *Wud yoo lighk t'plei with th'bawl?*
Мы идём в гости к бабушке.	We're going to visit Grandma. *Weer GOH-'ng t'VIZ-it GRAND-mah.*
Собирайся. Я собираюсь.	Get ready. I'm getting ready. *Get RED-ee. Ighm GET-'ng RED-ee.*

Я уже/ готов/ готова/:	I'm ready: *Ighm RED-ee:*
уходить, итти гулять,	to leave, to go for a walk, *t'leev, t'goh for uh wawk,*
есть (or) кушать.	to eat. *t'eet.*
Мы покажем ей, как ты быстро растёшь.	We'll show her how fast you're growing. *Weel shoh her haou fast yor GROH-'ng.*
Иди сюда (к маме).	Come here (to mommy). *Kuhm heer (t'MAHM-ee).*
Иди ко мне.	Come to me. *Kuhm t'mee.*
Смотри, как ты идёшь!	Look how you go! (walk) *Luk haou yoo goh! (wawk)*
Давай посмотрим, как ты умеешь ходить.	Let's see how you walk. *Letz see haou yoo wawk.*
Посмотри-ка на эти зубы!	Look at those teeth! *Luk at thohz teeth!*
У тебя болят зубы ?	Do your teeth hurt? *Doo yor teeth hert?*
Барабань в барабан!	Bang the drum! *Bang th'drum!*
Маршируй под музыку!	March to the music! *March t'th'MYOOZ-ik!*
Позвони в бубенчик!	Ring the bell! *Ring th'bel!*

39

Разговор_____

Какая красивая музыка!	What beautiful music! *Waht BYOOT-ih-ful MYOOZ-ik!*
Хлопай в ладоши!	Clap your hands! *Klap yor hanz!*
Сыграй другую песню!	Play another song! *Plei uh-NUTH-er sawng!*
Вот ребёнок, такой же как ты.	Here is a baby like you. *Heer iz uh BEI-bee lighk yoo.*
Кто это в зеркале?	Who is that in the mirror? *Hoo iz that in th'MEER-er?*
Где у ребёнка/ ножки/ глазки/?	Where are baby's/ feet/ eyes/? *Wehr ahr BEI-beez/ feet/ ighz/?*
Вот/ твой носик, ротик/ твоё ушко/.	Here is/ your nose, mouth/ ear/. *Heer iz/ yor nohz, maouth/ eer/.*
Давай прогуляемся в детской коляске.	Let's go for a stroll in your carriage. *Letz goh for uh strohl in yor KAR-ij.*
Нам нужно идти к врачу.	We have to go to the doctor. *Wee hav t'goh t'th DAHK-ter.*
Не бойся. Ничего страшного.	Don't be afraid. It's O.K. *Dohnt bee uh-FREID. Itz OH-kei.*
Ты боишься?	Are you afraid? *Ahr yoo uh-FREID?*
Я не боюсь.	I'm not afraid. *Ighm naht uh-FREID.*
Я иду за тобой!	I'm coming to get you! *Ighm KUHM-'ng t'get yoo!*

40

Поймал/-a!	Got-Cha! *GAHT-chah!*
Тебе нравится...(что-то)?	Do you like...(something)? *Doo yoo lighk... (SUHM-thng)?*
Разве ты не хочешь...+ infinitive?	Don't you want to... + infinitive? *Dohnt yoo wahnt too...?*
Разве ты не хочешь... + noun?	Don't you want... + noun? *Dohnt yoo wahnt...?*
Пойдём немного погуляем.	Let's take a little walk. *Letz teik uh LIT-ul wawk.*
Держись за мою руку.	Take my hand. *Teik migh hand.*
Сядь на свой стул.	Sit on your chair. *Sit ahn yor chehr.*
Не залезай на стул.	Don't climb up on the chair. *Dohnt klighm ahp ahn th'chehr.*
Смотри: ступенька.	Watch the step. *Wahtch th'step.*
Поднимись по лестнице.	Climb the stairs. *Klighm th'stehrz.*
Спускайся осторожно по лестнице.	Come down the stairs carefully. *Kuhm daoun th'stehrz KEHR-ful-ee.*
Держись за перила.	Hold on to the bannister. *Hohld ahn t'th'BAN-is-ter.*
Засунь ногу в штанину.	Put your foot in the pants. *Put yor fut in th'pantz.*
Вынь руку из рукава.	Pull your arm out of the sleeve. *Pul yor ahrm aout uv th'sleev.*

41

Папа поможет тебе надеть пижаму.	Daddy will help put on your pajamas. *DAD-ee wil help put ahn yor pah-JAH-mahz.*
Сходи и принеси свои новые туфли.	Go and get your new shoes. *Goh get yor noo shooz.*
Что у тебя в/ руке/ кармане/?	What do you have in your /hand/ pocket/? *Waht doo yoo hav in yor /hand/ PAHK-et/?*
Дай/ его/ её/ его/ мне.	Give it to me. *Giv it t'mee.*
Не трогай это. Это грязное.	Don't touch it. It's dirty. *Dohnt tuhch it. Itz DIRT-ee.*
Иди и возьми/ кубики / мяч/.	Go and get the/ blocks/ ball/. *Goh and get th'/blahks/ bawl/.*
Не сломай. * Не разбей.**	Don't break it. (toy)* (cup)** *Dohnt breik it. (toy) (kuhp)*
Не вставай. Сиди.	Don't get up. Stay seated. *Dohnt get ahp. Stei SEET-ed.*
Позаботься о мишке.	Take care of teddy. *Teik kehr uhv TED-ee.*
Дай/ ему/ ей/ чашку чая.	Give/ him/ her/ a cup of tea. *Giv/ him/ her/ uh kuhp uhv tee.*
Погладь собаку ласково.	Pet the dog gently. *Pet th'dawg JENT-lee.*
Не/ ударяй ногой/ ударяй/!	Stop/ kicking/ hitting/! *Stahp/ KIK-'ng/ HIT-'ng/!*
Не/ кусайся/ плачь/!	Stop/ biting/ crying/! *Stahp/ BIGHT-'ng/ KRIGH-'ng/!*

Остановись! Стой!	Stop! *Stahp!*
Вон отсюда! / Прочь! / Уходи!	Get out of here! Go away! *Get aout uhv heer! Goh uh-WEI!*
Мне так больно. (physical)	That hurts (me). *That hertz (mee).*
(Не) заходи.	(Don't) go in. *(Dohnt) goh in.*
Дай мне твою руку.	Give me your hand. *Giv mee yor hand.*
Ты очень шумишь!	You're making a lot of noise! *Yor MEIK-'ng uh laht uhv noiz!*
Кто кричит?	Who's shouting? *Hooz SHAOUT-'ng?*
Не кричи/ в доме/ в этой комнате/.	Don't shout/in the house/ in this room/. *Dohnt shaout/ in th'haous/* *in this room/.*
Тише! (or) Тихо!	Be quiet! *Bee KWIGH-et!*
Я сейчас занят/-а.	I'm busy now. *Ighm BIZ-ee naou.*
Я спешу. Поторопись!	I'm in a hurry. Hurry! *Ighm in uh HER-ee. HER-ee!*
У меня нет времени.	I have no time. *Igh hav noh tighm.*
/Нам/ Мне/ надо идти (уходить).	/We/ I/ must go (leave). */Wee/ Igh/ muhst goh (leev).*

Разговор_____

Я скоро вернусь.	I'll come back soon. *Ighl kuhm bak soon.*
Подожди! (меня)	Wait! (for me) *Weit! (for mee)*
Я подожду тебя.	I'll wait for you. *Ighl weit for yoo.*
Я тебя жду!	I'm waiting for you! *Ighm WEIT-'ng for yoo!*
Оставайся там.	Stay there. *Stei thehr.*
Не двигайся с места.	Don't move from that spot. *Dohnt moov fruhm that spaht.*
Не двигай (рукой).	Don't move (your hand). *Dohnt moov (yor hand).*
Мне бы хотелось, чтобы ты остался/ осталась /:	I would like you to stay: *Igh wud lighk yoo t'stei:*
в детской коляске,	in the carriage, *in th'KAR-ij,*
на кухне.	in the kitchen. *in th'KITCH-en.*
Я хочу, чтобы ты/ остался / осталась/ в своей комнате.	I want you to stay in your room. *Igh wahnt yoo t'stei in yor room.*
Подожди минуту, пожалуйста.	Just a moment, please. *Juhst uh MOH-ment, pleez.*
(Не) уходи.	(Don't) go away. *(Dohnt) goh uh-WEI.*
Уходи оттуда.	Come away from there. *Kuhm uh-WEI fruhm thehr.*

Перестань (так делать).	Stop doing that. *Stahp DOO-'ng that.*
Делай, что я тебе говорю!	Do what I tell you! *Doo waht igh tel yoo!*
Я же тебе говорил/-а!	What did I tell you! *Waht did igh tel yoo!*
Делай так, как тебе сказано!	Do as you are told! *Doo as yoo ahr tohld!*
Ты/ должен был/ должна была/ сказать мне об этом.	You should have told me about this. *Yoo shud hav tohld mee uh-BAOUT this.*
Я с тобой говорю!	I'm speaking to you! *Ighm SPEEK-'ng t'yoo!*
С кем ты говоришь?	To whom are you speaking? *Too hoom ahr yoo SPEEK-'ng?*
Что ты хочешь, чтобы я сделал/-а?	What do you want me to do? *Waht doo yoo wahnt mee t'doo?*
Не причиняй мне беспокойство.	Don't give me trouble. *Dohnt giv mee TRUH-bl.*
Не мешай мне сейчас.	Don't disturb me now. *Dohnt dis-TERB mee naou.*
Не дерись! Зачем вы спорите?	Don't fight! Why argue? *Dohnt fight! Wigh AHR-gyoo?*
О чём у тебя идёт спор?	What's the argument about? *Wahts th'AHR-gyoo-ment uh-BAOUT?*
Давай(те) по очереди.	Take turns. *Teik ternz.*

Разговор

Не беспокой/ его/ её/.

Don't bother/ him/ her/.
Dohnt BAH-ther/ him/ her/.

Не беспокой кошку.

Don't bother the cat.
Dohnt BAH-ther th'kat.

Не дразни его.

Don't tease him.
Dohnt teez him.

Не обращай на/ него/ неё/ внимания.

Don't pay any attention to
/ him/ her/.
Dohnt pei EN-ee uh-TEN-shuhn t'/him/ her/.

Оставь/ его/ её/ его/ в покое.

Leave/ him/ her/ it/ alone.
Leev/ him/ her/ it/ uh-LOHN.

Отстань от меня!

Leave me alone!
Leev mee uh-LOHN!

Не подбирай это.

Don't pick that up.
Dohnt pik that ahp.

/Открой/ Закрой/ дверь.

/Open/ Close/ the door.
/OH-pen/ Klohz/ th'dor.

Запри дверь (на замок).

Lock the door.
Lahk th'dor.

Не открывай окно.

Don't open the window.
Dohnt OH-pen th'WIND-oh.

Ты/ закрыл/-а /дверь/ окно/?

Did you close the/ door/ window/?
Did yoo klohz th'/dor/ WIND-oh/?

Не ложись на подоконник.

Don't lean on the window sill.
Dohnt leen ahn th'WIND-oh sil.

Положи коробку вон туда.

Put the box over there.
Put th'bahks OH-ver thehr.

(Не) прыгай!

(Don't) jump!
(Dohnt) jump!

Медленно!

Slowly!
SLOH-lee!

Не беги. Иди медленнее.

Don't run. Go slower.
Dohnt ruhn. Goh SLOH-er.

Иди как можно медленней.

Walk as slowly as possible.
Wawk as SLOH-lee as PAHS-ih-bl.

Ты оступишься.

You'll trip.
Yool trip.

Быстрее! Не спеши!

Hurry up! Don't hurry!
HER-ee ahp! Dohnt HER-ee!

Нам нужно спешить.

We must hurry.
Wee muhst HER-ee.

/Поставь/ Положи/ туфли на место.

Put the shoes back in their place.
Put th'shooz bak in thehr pleis.

Не пиши на стене.

Don't write on the wall.
Dohnt right ahn th'wawl.

Что это лежит/ на столе/ на полу/?

What is that lying on the /table /floor/?
Waht iz that LIGH-'ng ahn th/'TEI-bl/ flor/?

/Отойди на шаг/ Подойди на шаг/.

Step/ back/ forward/.
Step/ bak/ FOR-werd/.

Не трогай плиту.

Don't touch the range.
Dohnt tuhch th'reinj.

Ты обожжёшься!

You will burn yourself!
Yoo wil bern yor-SELF!

47

Ты/ обжёгся/ обожглась/?	Did you burn yourself? *Did yoo bern yor-SELF?*
Не играй со спичками!	Don't play with matches! *Dohnt plei with MACH-ez!*
Не зажигай спичку.	Don't light the match. *Dohnt light th'mach.*
Держись подальше от лестницы, барбекю, улицы.	Stay (Stand) away from the stairs, barbecue, street. *Stei (Stand) uh-WEI fruhm th' stehrz, BAR-bih-kwyoo, street.*
Не перебегай через улицу!	Don't run across the street! *Dohnt ruhn uh-KRAWS th'street!*
Держись за детскую коляску.	Hold on to the carriage. *Hohld ahn too th'KAR-ij.*
Посмотри/ налево/ направо/ перед тем, как переходить улицу.	Look /left/ right/ before crossing the street. *Luk/ left/ right/ bee-FOR KRAWS-'ng th'street.*
Подожди, когда зажжётся зелёный свет.	Wait for the green light. *Weit for th'green light.*
Впредь будь/ осторожен/ осторожна/!	From now on, be careful! *Fruhm naou ahn, bee KEHR-ful!*
Держи/ его/ её/ его/ на ручке/ обеими руками.	Hold it/ by the handle/ with both hands/. *Hohld it/ bigh th'HAND-le/ with bohth hanz.*
Обращай внимание на то, что ты делаешь.	Pay attention to what you are doing. *Pei uh-TEN-shuhn t'waht you ahr DOO-'ng.*

Не урони/ его/ её/ его/ на землю.

Don't drop it on the ground.
Dohnt drahp it ahn th'graound.

Что ты/ с ним/ с ней/ сделал/-а?

What did you do to it?
Waht did yoo doo too it?

Не порежь палец.

Don't cut your finger.
Dohnt kuht yor FING-er.

Нож острый.

The knife is sharp.
Th'NIGHF iz shahrp.

Не хватай это.

Don't grab that.
Dohnt grab that.

Как ты думаешь?

What do you think?
Waht doo yoo think?

...,потому что я так сказал/-а.

...because I say so.
...bee-KAWZ igh sei soh.

...,потому что это так.

...because that's the way it is.
...bee-KAWZ thatz th'wei it iz.

Из-за тебя...

Because of you...
Bee-KAWZ uhv yoo..

Ты думаешь что...?

Do you think that...?
Doo yoo think that..?

У меня (к тебе) большая просьба.

I have a favor to ask (of you).
Igh hav uh FEIV-er t'ask (uv yoo).

Принеси, пожалуйста, швабру.

Please bring me the mop.
Pleez bring mee th'mahp.

Ты не/ мог/ могла/ бы помочь мне приготовить обед?

Can you... (help me fix lunch)?
Kan yoo... (help mee fiks lunch)?

Разговор

Ты не/ мог/ могла/ бы отнести
это блюдо?

Can you carry the dish?
Kan yoo KAR-ee th'dish?

Ты бросил/-а камень?

Did you throw the stone?
Did yoo throh th'stohn?

Я/ видел/-а, как ты это сделал/-а.

I saw you do this.
Igh saw yoo doo this.

Могу ли я спросить тебя....?

May I ask you.........?
Mei igh ask yoo........?

Скажи брату, чтобы он пришёл
наверх.

Tell your brother to come upstairs.
*Tel yor BRUTH-er t'kuhm ahp-
STEHRZ.*

Скажи сестре, что я её ищу.

Tell your sister I'm looking
for her.
*Tel yor SIS-ter ighm LUK-'ng
for her.*

Поговори/ с ним/ с ней/
по-хорошему.

Speak to/ him/ her/ nicely.
Speek t'/him/ her/ NIGHS-lee.

Пусть/ он/ она/ скажет мне, что/
он/ она/ хочет.

Let/ him/ her/ tell me what
/ he/ she/ wants.
*Let/ him/ her/ tel mee waht
/ hee/ shee/ wants.*

Скажи ему, что ему нужно придти.

Tell him he should come.
Tel him hee shud kuhm.

Твоя сестра должна войти.

Your sister should come in.
Yor SIS-ter shud kuhm in.

Я хочу/ его/ её/ видеть.

I want to see/ him/ her/.
Igh want t'see/ him/ her/.

У тебя грязная рубашка.

Your shirt is dirty.
Yor shert iz DIRT-ee.

Иди в свою комнату и надень другую рубашку.	Go to your room, and put on another shirt. *Goh t'yor room, and put ahn uh-NUTH-er shert.*
Покажи мне, где твоя комната.	Show me where your room is. *Shoh mee wehr yor room iz.*
Что ты делаешь?	What are you doing? *Waht ahr yoo DOO-'ng?*
Ходи на цыпочках, когда ребёнок спит.	Tiptoe when baby is sleeping. *TIP-toh wen BEI-bee iz SLEEP-'ng.*
Ты можешь убаюкать ребёнка?	Can you rock the baby? *Kan yoo rahk th'BEI-bee?*
Не пугай/ его/ её/.	Don't scare/ him/ her/. *Dohnt skehr/ him/ her/.*
Сиди. Стой.	Remain/ seated/ standing/. *Ree-MEIN/ SEET-ed/ STAND-'ng/.*
/Сидите/ Встаньте/:	/Sit/ Stand/: */Sit/ Stand/:*
/поближе друг к другу/,	/ a little closer to each other/, */ uh LIT-ul KLOHS-er t'eech UH-ther/,*
/подальше друг от друга/.	/a little further from each other/. */ uh LIT-ul FURTH-er fruhm eech UH-ther/.*
Ты это сделал/-а? (назло)	Did you do it? (out of spite) *Did yoo doo it? (aout uv spight)*
Сделай по-моему.	Do it /the way I want /my way. *Doo it /th'wei igh wahnt/ migh wei.*

51

Я хочу, чтобы ты мне сказал/-а правду.

I want you to tell me the truth.
Igh wahnt yoo t'tel mee th'truth.

Посмотри мне прямо в глаза.

Look me straight in the eye.
Luk mee streit in th'igh.

Я хочу тебе кое-что сказать.

I want to tell you something.
Igh wahnt t'tel yoo SUHM-th'ng.

Расскажи мне об этом.

Tell me about it.
Tel mee uh-BAOUT it.

Говори/ медленнее/ яснее/.

Speak more/ slowly/ clearly/.
Speek mor/ SLOH-lee/ KLEER-lee/.

Говори как можно тише.

Speak as softly as possible.
*Speek as SAWFT-lee as
PAHS-ih-bl.*

Послушай внимательно.

Listen carefully.
LIS-en KEHR-ful-ee.

Послушай, что я хочу тебе сказать.

Listen to what I have to say.
LIS-en t'waht igh hav t'sei.

Что с тобой сегодня?

What's with you today?
Wahts with yoo tuh-DEI?

Со мной ничего.

Nothing's with me.
NUHTH-'ngz with mee.

Ты (сегодня) в/ плохом/ хорошем/ настроении.

You are in a/ bad/ good/ mood (today).
*Yoo ahr in uh/ bad/ gud/ mood
(tuh-DEI).*

Обещай хорошо себя вести!

Promise to be good!
PRAH-mis t'bee gud!

Я обещаю. Я бы не хотел/-а.

I promise. I'd rather not.
Igh PRAH-mis. Ighd RATH-er naht.

Я надеюсь, что ты будешь хорошо себя вести.

I expect you to be good.
Igh ek-SPEKT yoo t'bee gud.

Веди себя хорошо,...

Behave yourself,...
Bee-HEIV yor-SELF,...

...а то ты у меня (награды) не получишь!

...or you won't get any (reward)!
...or yoo woont get EN-ee (ree-WAWRD)!

Ты понимаешь, о чём я говорю?

Do you understand what I'm saying?
Doo yoo uhn-der-STAND waht ighm SEI-'ng?

Я думаю, что я понимаю, о чём ты говоришь.

I think I understand what you're saying.
Igh think igh uhn-der-STAND waht yor SEI-'ng.

Не выходи из себя.

Don't lose your temper.
Dohnt looz yor TEMP-er.

Понимаешь?

Do you understand?
Doo yoo uhn-der-STAND?

Будь послушным.

Don't be naughty.
Dohnt bee NAWT-ee.

Как ты упрям/-а!

Are you stubborn!
Ahr yoo STUHB-ern!

Не испытывай моё терпение!

Don't try my patience!
Dohnt trigh migh PEI-shens!

Не нервничай.

Don't be nervous.
Dohnt bee NER-vuhs.

Успокойся.

Calm down.
Kahm daoun.

53

Разговор

Всё будет в порядке.	Everything will be all right. *EV-ree-th'ng wil bee awl right.*
Покажи мне, где у тебя болит.	Show me where it hurts. *Shoh mee wehr it hertz.*
Ты упал/-а.	You fell. *Yoo fel.*
Ты/ ударился/ ударилась/ головой.	You have bumped your head. *Yoo hav bumpt yor hed.*
Потри рукой.	Rub it with your hand. *Rub it with yor hand.*
Открой рот.	Open your mouth. *OH-pen yor maouth.*
Не клади камешки в рот.	Don't put the pebble in your mouth. *Dohnt put th'PEB-le in yor maouth.*
Перестань строить рожи!	Stop making faces! *Stahp MEIK-'ng FEI-sez!*
Тебе же лучше будет.	That will do you good. *That wil doo yoo gud.*
Вытри свой нос.	Wipe your nose. *Wighp yor nohz.*
Дыши через нос.	Breathe through your nose. *Breeth throo yor nohz.*
Не говори мне, что...	Don't tell me that... *Dohnt tel mee that...*
Забудь о своей игрушке на мгновение.	Forget your toy for a moment. *For-GET yor toy for uh MOH-ment.*

У тебя уже их много.

You already have lots of them.
Yoo awl-RED-ee hav lahtz uhv them.

Играй со своими игрушками.

Play with your own toys.
Plei with yor ohn toyz.

Не трогай мои игрушки.

Don't touch my toys.
Dohnt tuhch migh toyz.

Я хочу всё!

' I want them all!
Igh wahnt them awl!

Не забудь (принести) цветные карандаши.

Don't forget (to bring) your crayons.
Dohnt for-GET yor KREI-ahnz.

Иди со мной.

Come with me.
Kuhm with mee.

Немедленно!

Immediately!
Ee-MEED-ee-et-lee!

Пойди первым.

You go first.
Yoo goh ferst.

Сюда. Иди за мной!

This way. Follow me!
This wei. FAHL-oh mee!

Ты думаешь, что ты можешь так сделать?

Do you think you can do it?
Doo yoo think yoo kan doo it?

Ты можешь так сделать?

Can you do that?
Kan yoo doo that?

Разве ты не можешь так сделать?

Can't you do that?
Kant yoo doo that?

Играй/ наверху/ внизу/.

Play/ upstairs/ downstairs/.
Plei/ ahp-STEHRZ/ DAOUN-stehrz.

Разговор

Иди/ наверх/ вниз/ помогать бабушке.	Go/ upstairs /downstairs /and help Grandma. *Goh/ ahp-STEHRZ/ DAOUN-stehrz and help GRAND-mah.*
Играй на тротуаре.	Play on the sidewalk. *Plei ahn th'SIGHD-wawk.*
Иди на улицу. Войди в дом.	Go outside. Come inside. *Goh aout-SIGHD. Kuhm in-SIGHD.*
/Включи/ Потуши/ свет.	Turn on/ Turn out/ the light. *Tern ahn/ Tern aout/ th'light.*
Зажги лампу.	Light the lamp. *Light th'lamp.*
Поставь видиокассету.	Put on the video. *Put ahn th'VID-ee-oh.*
Я не могу найти дорогу в темноте.	I can't find my way in the dark. *Igh kant fighnd migh wei in th'dark.*
Это твоё?	Is this yours? *Iz this yorz?*
Это (не) твоё.	This is (not) yours. *This iz (naht) yorz.*
Это моё? Это (не) моё.	Is this mine? This is (not) mine. *Iz this mighn? This iz (naht) mighn.*
Тебе не разрешено кушать в гостиной.	You are not allowed to eat in the living room. *Yoo ahr naht uh-LAOUD t'eet in th'LIV-'ng room.*

Ешь (Кушай) на кухне,	Eat in the kitchen, *Eet in th'KITCH-en,*
...чтобы не запачкать ковёр.	...so you don't stain the rug. *...soh yoo dohnt stein th'ruhg.*
Не спрашивай/ так часто/ больше/!	Don't ask /so often/ again/! *Dohnt ask/ soh AWF-en/ uh-GEN/!*
Не давай мне...	Don't give me... *Dohnt giv mee...*
Подожди, пока я приду.	Wait until I come back. *Weit un-TIL igh kuhm bak.*
(Потом) мы поговорим.	(Then) we'll talk. *(Then) weel tawk.*
Делай, что (ты) хочешь.	Do what you like. *Doo waht yoo lighk.*
Ты отвечаешь за своего маленького брата.	You're responsible for your brother. *Yor ree-SPAHN-sih-bl for yor BRUTH-er.*
Кто отвечает за...?	Who is responsible for...? *Hoo iz ree-SPAHN-sih-bl for...?*
Слушайся меня!	Obey me! *Oh-BEI mee!*
Иди в свою комнату!	Go to your room! *Goh t'yor room!*
Я был/-а у себя в комнате.	I was in my room. *Igh wuhz in migh room.*

Разговор

Не ссорьтесь друг с другом.	Don't quarrel with one another. *Dohnt KWAHR-el with wuhn* *uh-NUTH-er.*
Закрой холодильник.	Close the refrigerator. *Klohz th'ree-FRIJ-er-eit-er.*
Поставь масло в холодильник.	Put the butter in the refrigerator. *Put th'BUHT-er in th'* *ree-FRIJ-er-eit-er.*
Не торопись.	Take your time. *Teik yor tighm.*
Вытри туфли о половик.	Wipe your shoes on the mat. *Wighp yor shooz ahn th'mat.*
Сними свои туфли.	Remove your shoes. *Ree-MOOV yor shooz.*
Не ходи босиком!	Don't walk barefoot! *Dohnt wawk BEHR-fut!*
Что поделаешь? (Seemingly nothing)	What can we do? *Waht kan wee doo?*
Что бы нам поделать? (Activity with child)	What can we do? *Waht kan wee doo?*
Что мы можем сделать? (Offering help)	What can we do? *Waht kan wee doo?*
Давай попробуем вместе.	Let's try together. *Letz trigh tuh-GETH-er.*
Скажи мне, что (с тобой) случилось.	Tell me what happened (to you). *Tel mee waht HAP-end (t'yoo).*
Вот как это случилось.	It happened this way. *It HAP-end this wei.*

Не выражайся! (Swearing)	Do not use bad language! *Doo naht yooz bad LANG-wij!*
Ты всегда огрызаешься!	You have an answer for everything! *Yoo hav an AN-ser for EV-ree-th'ng!*
Я жду ответа.	I'm waiting for an answer. *Ighm WEIT-'ng for an AN-ser.*
Сделай радио потише.	Lower the radio. *LOH-er th'REID-ee-oh.*
Выключи телевизор.	Turn off the television set. *Tern awf th'TEL-ih-vij-uhn set.*
Тебе нельзя смотреть эту программу!	You may not watch that program! *Yoo mei naht wahch that PROH-gram!*
Приготовь уроки!	Do your lessons! *Doo yor LES-uhnz!*
Выключи телевизор, когда ты готовишь уроки.	No TV when you are doing lessons. *Noh tee-vee wen yoo ahr DOO-'ng LES-uhnz.*
Ты сделал/-а домашнюю работу?	Did you do your homework? *Did yoo doo yor hohm-werk?*
Перестань говорить по телефону!	Stop talking on the phone! *Stahp TAWK-'ng ahn th'fohn!*
О чём ты говоришь?	What are you talking about? *Waht ahr yoo TAWK-'ng uh-BAOUT?*

Разговор

/Я говорю/ Ты говоришь/ сам/-а с собой?

/Am I/ Are you/ talking to/ myself/ yourself/?
/Am igh/ Ahr yoo/ TAWK-'ng too/ migh-SELF/ yor-SELF/?

Перестань играть на компьютере!

Stop playing on the computer!
Stahp PLEI-'ng ahn th'kuhm-PYOOT-er!

Уже поздно приглашать твоих друзей.

It's too late to invite friends.
Itz too leit t'in-VIGHT frendz.

Книгу пора вернуть (в библиотеку).

Your book is due (at the library).
Yor buk iz doo (at th'LIGH-brer-ee).

Тебе нужно вернуть книгу в библиотеку.

You have to return the book to the library.
Yoo hav t'ree-TERN th'buk too th'LIGH-brer-ee.

Тебе нужно идти на занятия по музыке.

You have to go to your music lessons.
Yoo hav t'goh t'yor MYOO-zik LES-uhnz.

Пристегни ремень безопасности.

Fasten your seat belt.
FAS-en yor seet belt.

Из-за кого у нас так вырос счёт за телефон?

Who's been running up the phone bill?
Hooz ben RUHN'ng ahp th'fohn bil?

Ты/ должен/ должна/ покормить собаку.

You should feed the dog.
Yoo shud feed th'dawg.

Сейчас твоя очередь...

It's your turn ...
Itz yor tern...

выгуливать собаку,

to walk the dog,
t'wawk th'dawg,

выносить мусор.

to carry out the garbage.
*t'KAR-ee aout th'GAHR-
bij.*

Сними наушники!

Take off the head set!
Teik awf th'HED-set!

Приходи домой вовремя!

Come home on time!
Kuhm hohm ahn tighm!

Когда ты придёшь домой с
игровой площадки?

When will you come home from
the playground?
*Wen wil yoo kuhm hohm fruhm
th'PLEI-graound?*

Не опаздывай! Ты опаздал/-а!

Don't be late! You're late!
Dohnt bee leit! Yor leit!

Я боюсь, что уже слишком
поздно.

I'm afraid it's already too late.
*Ighm uh-FREID itz awl-RED-ee
too leit.*

Откуда ты идёшь?

Where are you coming from?
Wehr ahr yoo KUHM-'ng fruhm?

Я иду из своей комнаты.

I'm coming from my room.
Ighm KUHM'ng fruhm migh room.

Я вернусь домой вовремя.

I'll be home on time.
Ighl bee hohm ahn tighm.

Я всегда прихожу домой/ рано/
вовремя/.

I always come home/ early/
on time/.
*Igh AWL-weiz kuhm hohm/
ERL-ee/ ahn tighm/.*

Я не знаю, когда я приду домой.

I don't know when I'll be home.
Igh dohnt noh wen ighl bee hohm.

Разговор

Я не хочу слушать жалобы!	I don't want to hear any complaints! *Igh dohnt wahnt t'heer EN-ee kuhm-PLEINTZ!*
Об этом не может быть и речи!	That's out of the question! *Thatz aout uhv th'KWESH-chuhn!*

No sooner said than done.

Сказано – сделано

Помощь по дому   ## H<u>e</u>lping at Home

Your children are happiest when they are imitating adults in their lives. This includes the work they do. You and your children working together are a natural setting for speaking English together.

Помочь тебе (+ inf.)......?

Could I help you ......?
Kud igh help yoo....?

Помоги мне (+ inf.)...

Help me:
Help mee:

  накрыть на стол,

  set the table,
  set th'TEI-bl,

  пододвинуть этот стул
  (ближе к столу).

  move the chair (nearer
  the table).
  moov th'chehr (NEER-er
  th'TEI-bl).

Накрой на стол, пожалуйста.

Set the table, please.
Set th'TEI-bl, pleez.

Помощь по дому _____

Ты можешь положить салфетки
(на стол).

You can put the napkins on
(the table).
*Yoo kan put th'NAP-kinz ahn
(th'TEI-bl).*

Убери со стола, пожалуйста.

Clear the table, please.
Kleer th'TEI-bl, pleez.

Помоги мне/ помыть/ вытереть/
посуду.

Help me/ wash/ dry/ the dishes.
*Help mee/ wahsh/ drigh/
th'DISH-ez.*

Помоги мне постирать бельё.

Help me do the laundry.
Help mee doo th'LAWN-dree.

В раковине полно грязной
посуды.

The sink is filled with dirty dishes.
*Th'sink iz fild with DIR-tee
DISH-ez.*

Помоги мне/ убрать в доме/
убраться/.

Help me/ clean up around
the house/ clean up/.
*Help mee/ kleen ahp uh-
RAOUND th'haous/ kleen ahp/.*

Убирай всё!

Clean up everything!
Kleen ahp EV-ree-th'ng!

Помоги мне постелить постель.

Help me make the bed.
Help mee meik th'bed.

Помоги мне стирать.

Help me do the washing.
  (laundry)
*Help mee doo th'WAHSH'ng.
  (LAWN-dree)*

Ты постелил/-а кровать?

Did you make your bed?
Did yoo meik yor bed?

Почему нет?

Why not?
Wigh naht?

Ты заставляешь меня много работать!

You make me work a lot!
Yoo meik mee werk uh-LAHT!

Мама подметает пол.

Mommy's sweeping the floor.
MAH-meez SWEEP'ng th'flor.

Папа пылесосит коврик.

Daddy is vacuuming the rug.
DAD-ee iz VAK-yoom'ng th'ruhg.

Пылесос работает очень шумно.

The vacuum cleaner is noisy.
*Th'VAK-yoom KLEEN-er
iz NOYZ-ee.*

Какая пыль! Давай вытирать (пыль)!

What dust! Let's dust!
Waht dust! Letz duhst!

Держи тряпку в руке и три.

Hold the dust cloth in your hand, and rub.
*Hohld th'duhst klawth in yor
hand, and ruhb.*

Так, хорошо.

That's right.
Thatz right.

Я шью юбку для тебя.

I'm sewing a skirt for you.
Ighm SOH-'ng uh skert for yoo.

Помоги папе приготовить обед.

Help Daddy make lunch.
Help DAD-ee meik luhnch.

Мама печёт торт.

Mommy's baking a cake.
MAHM-eez BEIK-'ng uh keik.

Хочешь помочь мне печь печенье?

Do you want to help me bake cookies?
*Doo yoo wahnt t'help mee
beik KUK-eez?*

Насыпь муку.

Pour in the flour.
Poor in th'flaour.

65

Помощь по дому

Я взбиваю яйца.

I'm beating the eggs.
Ighm BEET-'ng th'eggz.

Мы смешиваем сахар и масло.

We mix the sugar and butter.
Wee miks th'SHUG-er n' BUHT-er.

Нам нужен разрыхлитель?

Do we need baking powder?
Doo wee need BEIK-'ng PAOUD-er?

Меси тесто как следует.

Knead the dough thoroughly.
Need th'doh THUHR-uh-lee.

Мы печём его в духовке.

We bake them in the oven.
Wee beik them in th'UH-vin.

Поставь часы на полчаса.

Set the clock for half an hour.
Set th'klahk for haf an aour.

Печенье готово.

The cookies are done.
Th'KUK-eez ahr duhn.

Ты не можешь мне помогать гладить.

You cannot help me iron.
Yoo KAN-naht help mee IGH-ern.

Ты можешь мне помочь сортировать и складывать одежду.

You can help me sort and fold the clothes.
Yoo kan help mee sort'n fohld th'klohz.

После уборки мы можем почитать рассказ.

After cleaning, we can read a story.
AF-ter KLEEN-'ng, wee kan reed uh STOR-ee.

Ты готов/-а читать со мной?

Are you ready to read with me?
Ahr yoo RED-ee t'reed with mee?

Убери кастрюли в шкаф.

Put the pots back in the cabinet.
Put th'pahts bak in th'KAB-in-et.

Перед тем как идти играть, тебе нужно убрать комнату.	Before playing, you must clean your room. *Bee-FOR PLEI- 'ng, yoo muhst KLEEN yor room.*
Ты хотел/-а бы пойти (со мной) по магазинам?	Would you like to go shopping (with me)? *Wud yoo lighk t 'goh SHAHP- 'ng (with mee)?*
Я хочу купить что-нибудь поесть.	I want to buy something to eat. *Igh wahnt t 'bigh SUHM-th 'ng t 'eet.*
Можно я пойду с тобой ?	May I come with you? *Mei igh kuhm with yoo?*
Ты можешь идти.	You may be excused. *Yoo mei bee ek-SKYOOSD.*
Что ты хочешь купить?	What do you want to buy? *Waht doo yoo wahnt t 'bigh?*
Мне нужно много разных вещей.	I need all kinds of things. *Igh need awl kighnz uhv th 'ngz.*
Вот тебе на твои расходы.	Here is your allowance. *Heer iz yor uh-LAOU-ens.*
Тебе нужно купить новую одежду.	You need to buy new clothes. *Yoo need t 'bigh noo klohz.*
Можешь помочь мне завернуть подарок?	Can you help me wrap the present? *Kan yoo help mee rap th 'PREZ-nt?*
Нам нужно сгрести снег.	We have to shovel the snow. *Wee hav t 'SHUHV-el th 'snoh.*
Помоги мне косить лужайку.	Help me mow the lawn. *Help mee moh th 'lawn.*

Помощь по дому_____

Сажай семена рядами.

Plant the seeds in a row.
Plant th'seedz in uh roh.

Здесь так много сорняков.

There are so many weeds.
Thehr ahr soh MEN-ee weedz.

Нам нужно прополоть сад...

We have to weed the garden...
Wee hav t'weed th'GAHRD-en...

...чтобы растения могли расти.

...so the plants will grow.
...soh th'plantz wil groh.

Ты будешь помогать мне поливать огород?

Will you help me water the
vegetable garden?
*Wil yoo help mee WAWT-er
th'VEJ-tuh-bl GAHRD-en?*

Не копай слишком/ много/ глубоко/.

Don't dig too/ wide/ deeply/.
Dohnt dig too/ wighd/ DEEP-lee/.

Копай здесь на клумбе.

Dig here in the flower bed.
Dig heer in th'FLAOU-er bed.

Осторожно, смотри: гусеницы!

Watch out for the caterpillars!
Wahch aout for th'KAT-er-pil-erz!

Помоги мне сгрести листья.

Help me rake the leaves.
Help mee reik th'leevz.

Брось листья в бак для мусора.

Throw the leaves in the
garbage pail.
*Throh th'leevz in th'GAHR-bij
peil.*

Положи разбрызгиватель здесь.

Put the sprinkler here.
Put th'SPRINK-ler heer.

Ты не можешь помогать мне обрезать деревья.

You cannot help me prune the trees.
*Yoo KAN-naht help mee proon
th'treez.*

Это слишком опасно.

It's too dangerous.
Itz too DEINJ-er-uhs.

Мы будем строить вагон.

We'll build a wagon.
Weel bild uh WAG-uhn.

Можешь ли ты очистить этот кусок дерева?

Can you sand this piece of wood?
Kan yoo sand this pees uhv wud?

Распили эту доску пополам.

Saw this board in two.
Saw this bord in too.

Вбей гвоздь.

Hammer the nail.
HAM-er th'neil.

Ты хочешь посмотреть?

Do you want to watch?
Doo yoo wahnt t'wahch?

Помоги мне чинить машину.

Help me work on the car.
Help mee werk ahn th'kahr.

/Помой/ Пропылесоси/ машину.

/Wash/ Vacuum/ the car.
/Wahsh/ VAK-yoom/ th'kahr.

Подмети тротуар.

Sweep the sidewalk.
Sweep th'SIGHD-wawk.

Помоги мне подключить компьютер.

Help me hook up the computer.
Help mee huk ahp th'kuhm-PYOOT-er.

Положи мои вещи на место.

Put my things back.
Put migh thingz bak.

Like teacher, like pupil.

Каков поп, таков и приход

Уроки в доме   School at Home

A popular trend is taking place in America where children and parents are taking charge of their own education. They are doing this at home. Children having classes at home instead of in a school building will find these phrases useful. Of course, these sentences will apply to a classroom situation as well.

Школьный автобус только что проехал!	The school bus just went by! *Th'skool buhs juhst went bigh!*
Нам пора начинать работать.	Time for us to start work. *Tighm for uhs t'start werk.*
Что мы будем делать сегодня?	What will we do today? *Waht wil wee doo tuh-DEI?*
Давайте (pl) будем точны.	Let's be punctual. *Letz bee PUHNK-chuh-wul.*

На чём мы (вчера) остановились? Where did we stop (yesterday)?
Wehr did wee stahp (YES-ter-dei)?

Какой сегодня день? What day is today?
Waht dei iz tuh-DEI?

Какой день будет завтра? What day is tomorrow?
Waht dei iz tuh-MAHR-oh?

Когда мы начнём нашу работу? When will we begin our work?
Wen wil wee bee-GIN aour werk?

Давайте продолжать работать. Let's go on working.
Letz goh ahn WERK-'ng.

Я/ рад/ рада/, что нам не нужно сегодня идти в школу. I'm glad we don't have to go to school today.
Ighm glad wee dohnt hav t'goh t'skool tuh-DEI.

Что ты изучаешь? What are you studying?
Waht ahr yoo STUHD-ee-'ng?

Я (сейчас) изучаю английский язык. I'm studying English.
Ighm STUHD-ee-'ng ING-lish.

Говори по-английски. Speak English.
Speek ING-lish.

Повторяй за мной. Repeat after me.
Ree-PEET AF-ter mee.

Зачем надо изучать русский язык? Why must we study Russian?
Wigh muhst wee STUHD-ee RUHSH-en?

Я/ рад/ рада/, что мы сегодня дома. I'm glad we're home today.
Ighm glad weer hohm tuh-DEI.

Уроки в доме

Этот проект о рыбах,	This fish project, *This fish PRAH-jekt,*
проект о картах,	map project, *map PRAH-jekt,*
проект о животных,	animal project, *AN-ih-mul PRAH-jekt,*
трудный/ труден.	is difficult. *iz DIF-ih-kuhlt.*
Время терпит.	There's plenty of time. *Thehrz PLEN-tee uhv tighm.*
Нам нужно:	We need: *Wee need:*
скотч, степлер,	scotch tape, a stapler, *skahch teip, uh STEIP-ler,*
ножницы, плакатный картон.	scissors, poster board. *SIZ-erz, POHST-er bord.*
Скобок нет.	There are no staples. *Thehr ahr noh STEIP-lerz.*
Как долго ты занимаешься математикой?	How long have you been working on math? *Haou lawng hav yoo ben WERK-'ng ahn math?*
Нам нужно изучать естественные науки?	Do we have to study science? *Doo wee hav t'STUHD-ee SIGH-ens?*
В котором часу мы начинаем уроки?	At what time are we starting lessons? *At waht tighm ahr wee START-'ng LES-uhnz?*

Мы будем заниматься/ утром/ днём/.

We'll study/ in the morning/ in the evening/.
Weel STUHD-ee/ in th'MORN-'ng/ in th'EEV-n'ng/.

Разве у тебя нет хорошей книги?

Don't you have a good book?
Dohnt yoo hav uh gud buk?

Тебе хочется почитать?

Do you feel like reading?
Doo yoo feel lighk REED- 'ng?

Мне сейчас нечего читать.

I have nothing to read.
Igh hav NUHTH- 'ng t'reed.

Мне сейчас не хочется это делать.

I don't feel like doing it now.
Igh dohnt feel lighk DOO'ng it naou.

Не ленись.

Don't be lazy.
Dohnt bee LEI-zee.

Скажи мне, если ты меня не поймёшь.

Tell me if you don't understand me.
Tel mee if yoo dohnt uhn-der-STAND mee.

Ты/ должен/ должна/ это знать.

You should know this.
Yoo shud noh this.

Тебе это понятно?

Does this make sense?
Duhz this meik sens?

Можно задать тебе вопрос?

Can I ask you a question?
Kan igh ask yoo uh KWESH-chun?

Помоги сестре в математике.

Help your sister with math.
Help yor SIS-ter with math.

Покажи сестре...

Show your sister...
Shoh yor SIS-ter...

...как ей делать математику.

...how to do her math.
...haou t'doo her math.

Математика для меня труднее,
а история легче.

Math is harder for me,
but history is easier.
Math iz HAHRD-er for mee,
but HIST-ree iz EEZ-ee-er.

Сложи эти цифры.

Add these figures.
Ad theez FIG-yurz.

Ты хочешь задать вопрос?

Do you want to ask a question?
Doo yoo wahnt t'ask uh
KWESH-chun?

Мама, у меня застрял дырокол.

Mom, the hole punch is stuck.
Mahm, th'HOHL puhnch iz stuhk.

Что тебе нужно?

What do you need?
Waht doo yoo need?

Тебе нужен карандаш?

Do you need a pencil?
Doo yoo need uh PEN-sil?

Тебе нужна книга?

Do you need a book?
Doo yoo need uh buk?

Тебе нужно зеркало?

Do you need a mirror?
Doo yoo need uh MEER-er?

Что мне делать? Мне скучно.

What is there for me to do?
I'm bored.
Waht iz thehr for mee t'doo?
Ighm bord.

Давайте (pl) сделаем небольшой
перерыв.

Let's take a little break.
Letz teik uh LIT-ul breik.

Мы будем работать в саду.

We'll work in the garden.
Weel werk in th'GARHD-en.

Когда мы вернёмся, мы

When we come back, we'll:
Wen wee kuhm bak, weel:

будем читать,

read,
reed,

подключимся к интернету,

go on-linc,
goh ahn-lighn,

пошлём кате электронную почту,

e-mail Katya,
EE-meil KAHT-yah,

испечём печенье для дяди Петра,

bake cookies for Uncle Peter,
beik KUK-eez for UHN-kl PEE-ter,

будем рисовать рисунок.

paint a picture.
peint uh PIK-chur.

Какого цвета цветы?

What color are the flowers?
Waht KUHL-er ahr th'FLAOUR-ez?

Нам нужно учиться.

We have to study.
Wee hav t'STUHD-ee.

Нам нужно писать

Do we have to have (to write)
Doo wee hav t'hav (t'right)

контрольную по истории,

a history quiz,
uh HIST-ree kwiz,

контрольную по географии?

a geography quiz?
uh jee-AHG-ruh-fee kwiz?

Я люблю учиться.

I like to study.
Igh lighk t'STUHD-ee.

Учи уроки.

Study your lessons.
STUHD-ee yor LES-uhnz.

Уроки в доме

Давай начинать урок.	Let's begin our lesson. *Letz bee-GIN aour LES-uhn.*
Занимайся своими уроками!	Get busy with your lessons! *Get BIZ-ee with yor LES-uhnz!*
Лучше я следующим делом приготовлю урок. (по истории)	I'd better do my (history) lesson next. *Ighd BET-er doo migh (HIST-ree) LES-uhn nekst.*
У тебя довольно времени это сделать.	You have enough time to do that. *Yoo hav ee-NUFF tighm t'doo that.*
Ты/ должен/ должна/ выучить это.	You've got to learn that. *Yoov gaht t'lern that.*
Постарайся сделать лучше.	Try to do better. *Trigh t'doo BET-er.*
Я помогу тебе как можно больше.	I will help you as much as possible. *Igh wil help yoo az muhch az PAHS-ih-bl.*
Мне нужно дополнительное время для музыки.	I need extra time for my music. *Igh need EK-struh tighm for migh MYOOZ-ik.*
Можно я пропущу урок истории?	May I skip history? *Mei igh skip HIST-ree?*
Мои цветные карандаши пропали.	My crayons are missing. *Migh KREI-ahnz ahr MIS-'ng.*
Ты их потерял/-а?	Have you lost them? *Hav yoo lawst them?*
Кто-нибудь их видел?	Has anyone seen them? *Haz EN-ee-wuhn seen them?*

Ты много работал/-а.	You have worked a lot. *Yoo hav werkt uh laht.*
Ты заслуживаешь что-нибудь приятное!	You deserve something nice! *Yoo duh-ZERV SUHM-th'ng nighs!*
Мне/ легко/ трудно/ (делать/ самому /самой /).	This is/ easy/ difficult/ for me (to do myself). *This iz/ EEZ-ee/ DIF-ih-kuhlt/ for mee (too doo migh-SELF).*
Как продвигается твоя работа?	How is your work coming along? *Haou iz yor werk KUHM'ng uh-LAWNG?*
Ты выучил/-а свой урок?	Do you know your lesson? *Doo yoo noh yor LES-uhn?*
Я учу урок.	I'm doing my lesson. *Ighm DOO-'ng migh LES-uhn.*
Я выучил/-а свой урок.	I know my lesson. *Igh noh migh LES-uhn.*
Я не выучил/-а своего урока.	I don't know my lesson. *I dohnt noh migh LES-uhn.*
Выброси ненужную бумагу в корзину.	Throw the waste paper in the basket. *Throh th'weist PEI-per in th' BASK-et.*

The end crowns the work.

Конец – Делу венец

Похвала   Praise

All the ways to say, "You're tops!" "None better!" "Wonderful, wonderful you!" and many, many more. Use this chapter *often*. You and your child will *LOVE* it.

Для меня ты лучше всех!	You're my number one! *Yor migh NUHM-ber wuhn!*
Какой красивый голос!	What a beautiful voice! *Waht uh BYOO-tih-ful voys!*
Ты хорошо/ ходишь/ чертишь/ поёшь/.	You/ walk/ draw/ sing/ well. *Yoo/ wawk/ draw/ sing/ wel.*
Как хорошо ты/ кушешь/ пишешь/ плаваешь/ играешь/!	How well you/ eat/ write/ swim/ play/! *Haou wel yoo/ eet/ right/ swim/ plei/!*

Ты удивительный/-ая!

You're wonderful!
Yor WUHN-der-ful!

Как ты/ мил/ мила/!

How (sweet) cute you are!
Haou (sweet) kyoot yoo ahr!

/Какой/-ая ты сильный/-ая!

How strong you are!
Haou strawng yoo ahr!

Какой/-ая смелый/-ая!

How brave you are!
Haou breiv yoo ahr!

Это платье тебе идёт.

This dress suits you.
This dres soots yoo.

Какие у теья красивые глаза!

What pretty eyes you have!
Waht PRIT-ee ighz yoo hav!

Я люблю/ твои глазки/ ручки/ пузик/.

I love/ your eyes/ hands/
your tummy/.
*Igh luv/ yor ighz/ hanz/ yor
TUHM-ee/.*

Ты выглядишь, как/ принцесса/ принц/.

You look like a /princess/ prince/.
Yoo luk lighk uh/ PRIN-ses/ prins/.

Ты хорошая девочка!

You are a good girl!
Yoo ahr uh gud girl!

Ты хороший мальчик!

You are a good boy!
Yoo ahr uh gud boy!

Ты/ добрый/ добрая/.

You are generous.
Yoo ahr JEN-er-uhs.

Будь всегда милым!

Always be nice!
AWL-weiz bee nighs!

Ты мне нравишся.

I like you.
Igh lighk yoo.

Похвала

Я тебя люблю.

I love you.
Igh luv yoo.

Браво! Бис!

Bravo! Encore! (Theatre)
BRAH-voh! AHN-kor!

Хорошо сделано! Ещё!

Well done! Again!
Wel duhn! Uh-GEN!

Мне нравится, что ты играешь тихо один.

I like the way you play quietly by yourself.
Igh lighk th'wei yoo plei KWIGH-et-lee bigh yor-SELF.

Попытайся ещё раз!

Try again!
Trigh uh-GEN!

Не сдавайся!

Don't give up!
Dohnt giv ahp!

Какая замечательная идея!

What a great idea!
Waht uh greit igh-DEE-uh!

Ты становишься лучше и лучше!

You're getting better and better!
Yor GET-'ng BET-er 'n BET-er!

Я/ благодарен/ благодарна/ тебе за твою помощь.

I am thankful for your help.
Igh am THANK-ful for yor help.

Ты был/-а терпелив/-а когда я говорил/-а по телефону.

You were patient while I was on the telephone.
Yoo wer PEI-shent wighl igh wuhz ahn th'tel-uh-fohn.

Это очень мило с твоей стороны.

That's kind of you.
Thatz kighnd uhv yoo.

Ты/ добрый/ добрая/!

You are kind!
Yoo ahr kighnd!

Ты уже убрал/-а в своей комнате.

You cleaned your room.
Yoo kleend yor room.

У тебя золотые руки.

You are good with your hands.
Yoo ahr gud with yor hanz.

Ты можешь гордиться собой!

You can be proud of yourself!
*Yoo kan bee praoud uhv
yor-SELF.*

All that glitters is not gold.

Не всё золото, что блестит

Покупки   ## Shopping

Shopping is a wonderful activity to familiarize you and your children with English vocabulary. Naming the items displayed in the stores and hearing others speaking English while they shop, will enable you to associate new words with their objects. You might want to "play store" at home to reenforce you and your child's English in the spirit of play.

Мне нужно составить список.	I have to make a list. *Igh hav t'meik uh list.*
Мне надо сходить за хлебом, молоком, мясом.	I need to buy bread, milk, meat. *Igh need t'bigh bred, milk, meet.*
Я еду в магазин за хлебом.	I'm driving to the store to get bread. *Ighm DRIGHV-'ng t'th stor t'get bred.*

Я собираюсь поехать:

I intend to go:
Igh in-TEND t'goh:

на склад лесоматериалов,

to the lumber yard,
t'th'LUHM-ber yahrd,

в питомник,

to the nursery,
t'th' NURS-ree,

на заправочную станцию,

to the gas station,
t'th' gas STEI-shen,

в магазин игрушек,

to the toy store,
t'th' toy stor,

в парикмахерскую,

to the barber shop,
t'th' BAHR-ber shahp,

в булочную,

to the bakery,
t'th BEIK-ree,

в гастроном,

to the grocery store,
t'th' GROHS-ree stor,

в прачечную,

to the laundromat,
t'th' LAWN-druh-mat,

в спортивный магазин,

to the sports store,
t'th' sportz stor,

в магазин деликатесов,

to the delicatessen,
t'th' del-ih-kuh-TES-en,

в универмаг,

to the department store,
t'th' dee-PAHRT-ment stor,

в аптеку,

to the drugstore,
t'th' DRUHG-stor,

в мясной магазин,

to the butcher shop,
t'th' BUCH-er shahp,

Покупки

в рыбный магазин,	to the fish store, *t'th' fish stor,*
в банк,	to the bank, *t'th' bank,*
в книжный магазин,	to the book store, *t'th' buk stor,*
в обувной магазин,	to the shoe store, *t'th'shoo stor,*
в музыкальный магазин,	to the music store, *t'th' MYOOZ-ik stor,*
в торговый центр,	to the mall, *t'th'mawl,*
на почту,	to the post office, *t'th pohst AWF-is,*
в видео магазин.	to the video store. *t'th VID-ee-oh stor.*
Я еду в супермаркет.	I am going to the supermarket. *Igh am GOH-'ng t'th'SOOP-er-mahr-ket.*
Здесь распродажа. Мне нужно купить...	There's a sale, here. I have to buy... *Thehrz uh seil, heer. Igh hav t'bigh...*
Где можно купить...?	Where can I buy...? *Wehr kan igh bigh...?*
Мне нужно вернуть...	I must return...(bring something back) *Igh muhst ree-TERN...(bring SUHM-th'ng bak)*

Что ты купишь в этом магазине?	What will you buy in this store? *Waht wil yoo bigh in this stor?*
Что ты купишь на свой доллар?	What will you buy with your dollar? *Waht wil yoo bigh with yor DAHL-er?*
Давай(те) поедим на/ лифте/ эскалаторе/.	Let's take the/ elevator/ escalator/. *Letz teik th'/EL-ih-veit-er/ ES-kuh-leit-er/.*
/Сиди/ Оставайся/ в тележке для покупок.	/Sit/ stay/ in the shopping cart. */Sit/ stei/ in th'SHAHP-'ng kahrt.*
Просунь ногу через отверстие.	Put your foot through the opening. *Put yor fut throo th'OHP-ning.*
Вы не могли бы помочь, пожалуйста?	Can you help me? *Kan yoo help mee?*
Что-нибудь ещё?	Anything else? *EN-ee-th'ng else?*
Нам нужно купить новую одежду.	We need to buy new clothes. *Wee need t'bigh noo klohz.*
Я хочу купить:	I want to buy: *Igh wahnt t'bigh:*
что-нибудь/ хорошее/ симпатичное/,	something/ nice/ pleasant/, *SUHM-th'ng/ nighs/ PLEZ-ent,*
что-нибудь новое,	something new, *SUHM-th'ng noo,*
что-то белое.	something white. *SUHM-th'ng wight.*

Мне хотелось бы...	I'd like... *Ighd lighk...*
Нам нельзя истратить все свои деньги.	We cannot spend all our money. *Wee KAN-naht spend awl aour MUHN-ee.*
Мы не можем это купить.	We cannot buy that. *Wee KAN-naht bigh that.*
Я осталась (почти) без денег.	I'm (almost) out of money. *Ighm (AWL-mohst) aout uhv MUHN-ee.*
Сколько у тебя при себе денег?	How much money do you have? (on you) *Haou muhch MUHN-ee doo yoo hav? (ahn yoo)*
Это слишком много денег.	That's too much money. (to be carrying) *Thatz too muhch MUHN-ee.*
У меня нет денег.	I have no money. *Igh hav noh MUHN-ee.*
У меня/ немного/ много/ денег.	I have/ a little/ a lot of/ money. *Igh hav/ uh LIT-ul / uh laht uhv/ MUHN-ee.*
Копи свои деньги.	Save your money. *Seiv yor MUHN-ee.*
Это слишком дорого.	That's too expensive. *Thatz too ek-SPEN-siv.*
Может быть, что-нибудь подешевле.	Perhaps something cheaper. *Per-HAPZ SUHM-th'ng CHEEP-er.*
Это/ удачная/ неудачная/ покупка.	That's a/ good/ poor/ buy. *Thatz uh/ gud/poor/ bigh.*

Мне нужно денег.	I need some money. *Igh need suhm MUHN-ee.*
/Продавец/ Продавщица/ там.	The /salesman/ saleswoman/ is over there. *Th'/SEILZ-m'n/ SEILZ-* *WUM-en/ iz OH-ver thehr.*
Сколько это стоит?	How much is it? *Haou muhch iz it?*
Сколько с меня?	How much do I owe you? *Haou muhch doo igh oh yoo?*
Нам нужно это купить?	Should we buy it? *Shud wee bigh it?*
Стоит ли нам это покупать?	Should we buy it? *Shud wee bigh it?*
Давай купим/ его/ её/ для мамы.	Let's buy it for mother. *Letz bigh it for MUTH-er.*
Не покупай это.	Don't buy that. *Dohnt bigh that.*
Я покупаю/ его/ её/ их/.	I'm buying/ it/ them/. *Ighm BIGH-'ng /it/ them/.*
Какого размера это пальто?	What size is this coat? *Waht sighz iz this koht?*
Какой это размер?	What size is it? *Waht sighz iz it?*
Дай мне посмотреть.	Let me see that. *Let mee see that.*
Примерь.	Try it on. *Trigh it ahn.*

Покупки

Какой/ Какая/ тебе больше нравится?	Which do you prefer? *Wich doo yoo pree-FER?*
/Этот/ Эта/ Это/ слишком/ –	This is too – *This iz too –*
– узок/ узка/ узко/.	– tight, *tight,*
– просторен / просторна / просторно/.	– loose. *loos.*
Это пальто тебе/ велико/ мало/.	This coat is/ large/ small/ for you. *This koht iz/ lahrj/ smawl/ for yoo.*
Эта шляпа тебе/ велика/ мала/.	This hat is/ large/ small/ for you. *This hat iz/ lahrj/ smawl/ for yoo.*
Этот свитер тебе/ велик/ мал/.	This sweater is/ large/ small/ for you. *This SWET-er iz/ lahrj/ smawl/ for yoo.*
/Он /Она /Оно/ на тебе превосходно сидит.	It fits (you) perfectly. *It fitz (yoo) PER-fekt-lee.*
Тебе очень идёт.	It looks good on you. *It lukz gud ahn yoo.*
Посчитай сдачу.	Count your change. *Kaount yor cheinj.*
Где мы с тобой встретимся?	Where shall we meet? *Wehr shal wee meet?*
Встречаемся здесь через час.	Meet me here in an hour. *Meet mee heer in an aour.*

Будь рядом/ со мной/ с мамой/ с папой/.

Stay near/ me/ Mom/ Dad/.
Stei neer/ mee/ mahm/ dad/.

Как ты думаешь, папе понравится?

Do you think Dad would like it?
Doo yoo think dad wud lighk it?

У вас есть хозяйственная сумка?

Do you have a shopping bag?
Doo yoo hav uh SHAHP-'ng bag?

Магазин полон народу.

The store is crowded.
Th'stor iz KRAOUD-ed.

Не иди у меня за спиной.

Don't walk behind me.
Dohnt wawk bee-HIGHND mee.

Где касса?

Where is the cashier?
Wehr iz th'KASH-eer?

Следующий!

Next!
Nekst!

Мы можем просто побродить по магазинам.

We can go window shopping.
Wee kan goh WIND-oh SHAHP'-ng.

/Выход / Вход/ там.

/The exit/ entrance/ is over there.
/The EG-zit/ EN-trens/ iz OH-ver thehr.

Мы ищем/ игрушки/ мебель / одежду/.

We're looking for/ toys/ furniture/ clothing/.
Weer LUK-'ng for/ toyz/ FERN-ih-cher/ KLOH-th'ng/.

Стоянка запрещена!

No parking!
Noh PAHRK-'ng!

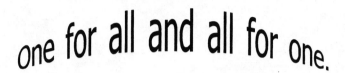

Один за всех, все за одного

Весело!   Fun !

If this chapter's pages don't have paint stains, water marks, and gum sticking the pages together, you are not getting all there is to wring out of these pages! Be sure to add some of your sentences that are appropriate. I have found it helpful to place sentences and phrases on 3 x 5 cards wherever I need them until the phrase is part of my thinking.

Можно мне пойти на улицу?	Can I go outside? *Kan igh goh AOUT-sighd?*
Можешь/ тебе разрешается/:	You/ can/ are allowed to/ may/: *Yoo/ kan/ ahr uh-laoud t'/mei/:*
поиграть во дворе,	play in the yard, *plei in th'yahrd,*
пойти на детскую площадку,	go to the playground, *goh t' th'PLEI-graound,*

пойти на (футбольное, бейсбольное) поле,	go to the (soccer, baseball) field , *goh t'th (SAHK-er, BEIS-bawl) feeld,*
сходить/ к своему другу/ к своей подруге/.	go to your friend's house. *goh t'yor frendz haous.*
Спроси их, хотят ли они поиграть:	Ask them if they want to play: *Ask them if thei wahnt t'plei:*
во врача и медсестру,	doctor and nurse, *DAHK-ter and nurs,*
в магазин,	shopkeeper, *SHAHP-keep-er,*
на компьютере,	computer, *kuhm-PYOOT-er,*
в прятки.	hide and seek. *highd and seek.*
Можно/ с тобой / с вами/ поиграть?	May I play with you? *Mei igh plei with yoo?*
Можно мне тоже прийти?	May I come, too? *Mei igh kuhm, too?*
Я/ больше/ выше/ тебя.	I'm/ bigger/ taller/ than you. *Ighm/ BIG-er/ TAWL-er/ than yoo.*
Я сильнее тебя.	I'm stronger than you. *Ighm STRAWNG-er than yoo.*
Я старше тебя.	I'm older than you. *Ighm OHLD-er than yoo.*

Моя собака лучше твоей.	My dog is nicer than yours. *Migh dawg iz NIGHS-er than yorz.*
Мой велосипед лучше твоего.	My bike is better than yours. *Migh bighk iz BET-er than yorz.*
Моя комната лучше твоей.	My room is better than yours. *Migh room iz BET-er than yorz.*

САМОЛЁТЫ — AIRPLANES
AEHR-pleinz

Пилот диспетчеру.	Pilot to tower. *PIGH-lut t'TAOUR.*
Пожалуйста, пристегните ремни безопасности.	Please fasten your seat belt. *Pleez FAS-en yor seet belt.*
Вылетаю!	I'm taking off! *Ighm TEIK-'ng awf!*
Сбавить газ!	Throttle down! *THRAHT-le daoun!*
Я иду на посадку!	I'm landing! *Ighm LAND-'ng!*
У нас заканчивается топливо!	We're running out of fuel! *Weer RUHN'ng aout uhv fyool!*
Очистить взлётную полосу!	Clear the runway! *Kleer th'RUHN-wei!*
Сколько времени лететь до Москвы?	How long is the flight to Moscow? *Haou lawng iz th'flight t'MAHS-kaou?*

ВО ДВОРЕ/ В САДУ — IN THE YARD/ GARDEN
In th' yahrd/ GAHRD-en

Иди и играй/ на улице/ дома/.	Go/ outside/ inside /and play. *Goh/ AOUT-sighd/ IN-sighd/ and plei.*
Играй/ во дворе /в песочнице/.	Play in the/ yard/ sandbox/. *Plei in th'/yahrd/ SAND-bahks/.*
Ты хочешь пускать мыльные пузыри?	Do you want to blow bubbles? *Doo yoo wahnt t'bloh BUHB-uhlz?*
Не играй в грязи.	Don't play in the dirt. *Dohnt plei in th'dirt.*
Не рви цветы, пожалуйста!	Please don't pick the flowers! *Pleez dohnt pik th'FLAOU-erz!*
Можешь плавать в бассейне, если я с тобой.	You can swim in the pool if I am with you. *Yoo kan swim in th'pool if igh am with yoo.*
Прыгни с вышки, как я тебе показывал/-а.	Jump off the diving board as I've shown you. *Jump awf th' DIGHV-'ng bord az ighv shohn yoo.*
Будь/ осторожен/ осторожна/, когда ты взбираешь на дерево.	Be careful when you are climbing the tree. *Bee KEHR-ful wen yoo ahr KLIGHM-'ng th'tree.*
Вы оба можете сидеть в вагоне.	You both can sit in the wagon. *Yoo bohth kan sit in th'WAG-uhn.*
Здесь достаточно места для двоих.	There's enough room for two. *Thehrz ee-NUFF room for too.*

Весело!
_____

Не уходи со двора.

Don't leave the yard.
Dohnt leev th'yahrd.

БЕЙСБОЛ — BASEBALL
BEIS-bawl

Твоя очередь (бить битой).

It's your turn (at bat).
Itz yor tern (at bat).

Лови! Бросай!

Catch! Throw!
Kach! Throh!

Держи биту за собой.

Hold the bat behind you.
Hohld th'bat bee-highnd yoo.

Следи за мячом.

Keep your eye on the ball.
Keep yor igh ahn th'bawl.

Ударяй (битой).

Swing (with the bat).
Swing (with th'bat).

Не попал/-а по мячу.
Мимо!

You missed the ball. Missed!
Yoo mist th'bawl. Mist!

Ты выиграл/-а пробег!

You scored a run!
Yoo skord uh ruhn!

Это был хороший бросок!

That was a good throw!
That wuhz uh gud throh!

ЕЗДА НА ВЕЛОСИПЕДЕ — BICYCLING
BIGH-sih-kling

Поставь ноги на педали.

Put your feet on the pedals.
Put yor feet ahn th'PED-uhlz.

Не крути так быстро педали.

Don't pedal so fast.
Dohnt PED-ul soh fast.

У тебя/ держу/ придерживаю/.

I've got a hold of you.
(firmly/ lightly)
Ighv gaht uh hohld uhv yoo.

Старайся поддерживать
равновесие.

Try to keep your balance.
Trigh t'keep yor BAL-ens.

Дай я попробую!

Let me try!
Let mee trigh!

Держись за руль!

Hold on to the handlebars!
Hohld ahn too th'HAND-uhl-bahrz!

Поезжай прямо.

Go straight.
Goh streit.

Поезжай/ направо/ налево/.

Go/ right/ left/.
Goh/ right/ left/.

Крути педали!

Keep pedaling!
Keep PED-uhl-'ng!

Ты очень хорошо едешь на
велосипеде.

You're riding your bicycle
very well.
*Yor RIGHD-'ng yor BIGH-sih-
kuhl VER-ee wel.*

Не езди на велосипеде по улице!

Don't ride your bicycle in the
street!
*Dohnt righd yor BIGH-sih-kuhl
in th'street.*

Там слишком сильное движение.

There's too much traffic.
Thehrz too muhch TRAF-ik.

Ты едешь слишком быстро!

You're going too fast!
Yor GOH-'ng too fast!

Весело!

Нажми на тормоз!

Put on the brake!
Put ahn th'breik!

Не свались с велосипеда.

Don't fall off your bicycle.
Dohnt fawl awf yor BIGH-sih-kuhl.

Ты/ свалился/ свалилась/
с велосипеда.

You fell off your bicycle.
Yoo fel awf yor BIGH-sih-kuhl.

Тебе нужно надеть шлем.

You need to put on your helmet.
Yoo need t'put ahn yor HELM-uht.

НАСТОЛЬНЫЕ ИГРЫ — BOARD GAMES
Bord geimz

Ты хочешь поиграть/ в шашки/
в шахматы / в настольную игру/?

Do you want to play/ checkers
/ chess/ a board game/?
*Doo yoo wahnt t'plei/ CHEK-erz
/ches/ uh bord geim/?*

Чья очередь?

Whose turn is it?
Hooz tern iz it?

Опять моя (твоя) очередь.

It's my (your) turn again.
Itz migh (yor) tern uh-GEN.

Я брошу кубики.

I'll throw the dice.
Ighl throh th'dighs.

Я хочу синюю фигуру.

I want the blue figure. (piece)
Igh wahnt th'bloo FIG-yur.

Твоя фигура не на том месте.

Your piece is in the wrong place.
Yor pees iz in th'rawng pleis.

Ты не так идёшь.

You're going the wrong way.
Yor GOH-'ng th'rawng wei.

Пойди/ вперёд/ назад/.	Move/ forward/ backward/. _Moov/ FOR-werd/ BAK-werd/._
Ты не честно играешь.	You aren't playing fairly. _Yoo AHR-ent PLEI-'ng FEHR-lee._
Ты/ должсн/ должпа/ мне заплатить.	You have to pay me. _Yoo hav t'pei mee._
Ты мне/ должен/ должна/.	You owe me money. _Yoo oh mee MUHN-ee._
Я заплачу.	I'll pay. _Ighl pei._
Ты/ выиграл/-а/ проиграл/-а.	You have/ won/ lost/. _Yoo hav /wuhn/ lawst/._

ЛОДКИ — BOATS
Bohts

Корабль отправляется!	All aboard! _Awl uh-BORD!_
Мы уезжаем из порта.	We're leaving port. _Weer LEEV-'ng port._
Мы идём в плавание в Россию.	We're sailing to Russia. _Weer SEIL-'ng t'RUSH-uh._
Лодка тонет!	The boat is sinking! _Th'boht iz SINK-'ng!_
Человек за бортом!	Man overboard! _Man OH-ver-bord!_
Покиньте корабль!	Abandon ship! _Uh-BAND-uhn ship!_

Спускайте спасательную шлюпку!	Lower the life boats! *LOH-er th'LIGHF bohtz!*
Мы едем кататься на лодке.	We're going boating. *Weer GOH- 'ng BOHT- 'ng.*
Помедленнее!	Slow down! *Sloh daoun!*
Я буду управлять лодкой.	I'll drive the boat. *Ighl drighv th'boht.*
Ты можешь кататься на водных лыжах.	You can water-ski. *Yoo kan WAWT-er-skee.*
Выйди и оттолкни!	Get out and push off! *Get aout 'n push awf!*
Сходи за вёслами!	Get the oars! *Get th'orz!*
Я погребу. (or) Я буду грести.	I'll row. *Ighl roh.*
Греби как можно быстрее.	Row as fast as you can. *Roh az fast az yoo kan.*

ПОХОД — CAMPING
KAMP- 'ng

Сколько времени мы хотим стоять лагерем?	How long do we want to camp? *Haou lawng doo wee wahnt t'kamp?*
Нам нужна новая палатка.	We need a new tent. *Wee need uh noo tent.*
Я/ рад/ рала/,что у нас есть наш фургон.	I am happy that we have our camper. *Igh am HAP-ee that wee hav aour KAMP-er.*

98

Давайте поставим палатку.

Let's pitch the tent
Letz pich th'tent.

Я хочу, чтобы лагерь стоял прямо на озере.

I want a camp site right on the lake.
Igh wahnt uh kamp sight ahn th'leik.

Положи свой спальный мешок в палатку.

Put your sleeping bag inside the tent.
Put yor SLEEP-'ng bag IN-sighd th'tent.

Установи плитку.

Set up the stove.
Set ahp th'stohv.

Это идеальное место для лагеря.

This is a perfect place to camp.
This iz uh PERF-ekt pleis t'kamp.

МАШИНЫ — CARS
Kahrz

Машина сломалась.

The car broke down.
Th'kahr brohk daoun.

Она дальше не едет.

It doesn't go any more.
It DUHZ-ent goh EN-ee mor.

Почему машина не едет?

Why doesn't the car go?
Wigh DUHZ-ent th'kahr goh?

Подтолкни машину. Я поведу.

Push the car. I'll drive.
Push th'kahr. Ighl drighv.

Проверьте, пожалуйста, масло, воду, аккумулятор.

Check the oil, the water, the battery, please.
Chek th'oyl, th'WAWT-er, th'BAT-er-ee, pleez.

Весело!

Заправьте машину!	Fill 'er up! *Fil-er ahp!*
Заведи машину в гараж.	Drive the car into the garage. *Drighv th'kahr IN-too th'* *gah-RAHJ.*
Дай задний ход.	Back up. *Bak ahp.*
Быстро! Дай газу!	Step on it! Give it the gas! *Step ahn it! Giv it th'gas!*
Посигналь! Нажми на сигнал!	Honk! Blow the horn! *Hahnk! Bloh th'horn!*
Мой любимый автомобиль.........	My favorite car is..... *Migh FAV-or-it kahr iz....*

РАСКРАСЬ И ПРИКЛЕЙ — COLOR and PASTE
KUHL-er 'n peist

Ей можно взять цветные карандаши.	She may use the crayons. *Shee mei yooz th'KREI-ahnz.*
Раскрась солнце жёлтым цветом.	Color the sun yellow. *KUHL-er th'suhn YEL-oh.*
Нарисуй птицу каким хочешь. цветом	Paint the bird the color you like. *Peint th'bird th'KUHL-er yoo lighk.*
Вырежи эту картинку из журнала.	Cut this picture out of the magazine. *Kuht this PIK-cher aout uhv th'* *mag-uh-ZEEN.*
Приклей картинку на бумагу (клейкой лентой).	Tape the picture on the paper (with sticky tape). *Teip th'PIK-cher ahn th'* *PEI-per (with STIK-ee teip).*

Приклей это осторожно на бумагу.	Paste this carefully on the paper. *Peist this KEHR-ful-ee ahn th'PEI-per.*
Сложи лист бумаги.	Fold the paper. *Fohld th'PEI-per.*
Не порви бумагу.	Don't tear the paper. (Be careful.) *Dohnt tehr th'PEIP-er. (Bee KEHR-ful.)*
Собери клочки бумаги.	Pick up the scraps of paper. *Pik ahp th'skraps uhv PEI-per.*
Нарисуй:	Draw: *Draw:*
круг,	the circle, *th'SIRK-ul,*
треугольник,	the triangle, *th'TRIGH-ang-ul,*
прямоугольник,	the rectangle, *th'REK-tang-ul,*
и квадрат (вот так).	and the square (like this). *and th'skwehr (lighk this).*
/Раскатай/ Разомни/ глину.	/Roll/ Knead/ the clay. */Rohl/ Need/ th'klei.*

КОМПЬЮТЕР — COMPUTER
Kuhm-PYOOT-er

Ты хочешь поиграть в компьютерную игру?	Do you want to play a computer game? *Doo yoo wahnt t'plei uh kuhm-PYOOT-er geim?*

Мы это разпечатаем.

We'll print it out.
Weel print it aout.

Это неправильное сообщение.

There's an error message.
Thehrz an EHR-er MES-ij.

Мы можем осуществить поиск
на компьютере.

We can make a computer
search.
Wee kan meik uh kum-PYOOT-er serch.

КУКЛЫ — DOLLS
Dahlz

Как зовут твою куклу?

What is your doll's name?
Waht iz yor dahlz neim?

Твоя кукла красивая?

Is your doll pretty?
Iz yor dahl PRIT-ee?

Покорми свою куклу.

Feed your doll.
Feed yor dahl.

Одень куклу.

Dress the doll.
Dres th'dahl.

Мне нужно её причесать.

I have to comb her hair.
Igh hav t'kohm her hehr.

Положи её аккуратно.

Put her down gently.
Put her daoun JENT-lee.

Не шлёпай куклу так сильно!

Don't spank the doll so hard!
Dohnt spank th'dahl soh hard!

Ты можешь сделать модель платья
на компьютере.

You can design a dress on the
computer.
*Yoo kan d'ZIGHN uh dres
ahn th'kuhm-PYOOT-er.*

УГАДАЙ — GUESS WHAT !
Ges waht!

Мне нравятся красные плащи. Я большой. Я нападаю с помощью рогов. Какое я животное? (бык)

I like red capes. I'm large. I charge with my horns. What **a**nimal am I? (bull)

Я сижу на кувшинках. Я говорю: "Ква-ква!" Я ловлю насекомых языком. Какое я животное? (лягушка)

I sit on w**a**ter-lilies. I say, "Croak!Croak!" I catch **i**nsects with my tongue. Which **a**nimal am? (frog)

Я лаю, рычу и гоняю кошек. Я говорю: "Гав-гав!" Какое я животное? (собака)

I bark, growl and chase cats. I say, "Bow-wow"! Which **a**nimal am I? (dog)

Я ношу детёнышей в сумке. У меня четыре лапы; но я не умею бегать. Я прыгаю. Какое я животное? (кенгуру)

I c**a**rry my young in my pouch. I have four legs; I cann**o**t run. I hop.Which **a**nimal am I? (kangar**oo**)

Я хожу величественно и кукарекаю. У меня есть перья. Я говорю: "Кукареку!" Какое я животное? (петух)

I strut and crow. I have f**ea**thers. I say, "Cock-a-d**oo**dle-doo!" Which **a**nimal am I? (r**oo**ster)

ДЕТСКАЯ ПЛОЩАДКА — PLAYGROUND
PLEI-graound

Иди и прячься!

Go and hide!
Goh 'n highd!

Смывайся! Сматывайся!

Scram!
Skram!

Где ты? Где я?

Where are you? Where am I?
Wehr ahr yoo? Wehr am igh?

Я здесь! (or) Вот и я!

Here I am!
Heer igh am!

Весело!

Давай качаться на качелях!	Let's swing on the swing! *Letz swing ahn th'swing!*
Не прыгай с качелей!	Don't jump off the swing! *Dohnt jump awf th'swing!*
Не стой (ногами) на качелях!	Don't stand on the swing! *Dohnt stand ahn th'swing!*
Не качайся на качелях стоя на ногах.	Don't swing while standing. *Dohnt swing wighl STAND-'ng.*
Я тебя слегка раскачиваю.	I am pushing you gently. *Igh am PUSH-'ng yoo JENT-lee.*
Не закрывай глаза!	Don't close your eyes! *Dohnt klohz yor ighz!*
Держись за/ поручни горки/ каруселей/.	Hold on to the /slide/ merry-go-round/. *Hohld ahn too th'/ slighd/ MER-ee-goh-raound/.*
Спускайся с горки!	Slide down the slide! *Slighd daoun th'slighd!*
Воздушный змей падает.	The kite is falling. *Th'kight iz FAWL-'ng.*
Не достаточно сильный ветер.	There's not enough wind. *Thehrz naht ee-NUFF wind.*
Держи верёвку крепко!	Hold the tail tightly! *Hohld th'teil TIGHT-lee!*
Хочешь скакалку?	Do you want to jump rope? *Doo yoo wahnt t'jump rohp?*
Стреляй стеклянными шариками в круг.	Shoot the marbles into the circle. *Shoot th'MAHR-bulz IN-too th'SIRK-ul.*

Надуй воздушный шарик.	Blow up the balloon. *Bloh ahp th'buh-LOON.*
Шарик сдувается!	Air is leaking from the balloon! *Ehr iz LEEK-'ng fruhm th'buh-* *LOON!*
Помоги! Пожар! Включи сирену!	Help! Fire! Sound the siren! *Help! Fighr! Saound th'SIGHR-en!*
Позвони в пожарное отделение!	Call the fire department! *Kawl th'fighr dee-PAHRT-ment!*
Следуй за лидером!	Follow the leader! *FAHL-oh th'LEED-er!*
Встаньте (pl.) в круг.	Stand in a circle. *Stand in uh SIRK-uhl.*
Коньки затупились.	My skates are dull. *Migh skeits ahr duhl.*
Их нужно поточить.	They need to be sharpened. *Thei need t'bee SHAHRP-end.*
Держись за меня. Я тебе помогу.	Hold on to me. I'll help you. *Hohld ahn t'mee. Ighl help yoo.*
Отталкивайся с левой ногой.	Push off with your left foot. *Push awf with yor left fut.*
Подними правую ногу.	Lift the right foot. *Lift th'right fut.*
Прокатись на коньках вокруг катка.	Skate around the rink. *Skeit uh-RAOUND th'rink.*
Ты готов/-а кататься на коньках спиной.	You're ready to skate backwards. *Yor RED-ee t'skeit BAK-werdz.*

ФУТБОЛ — SOCCER
SAHK-er

Веди мяч!

Dribble the ball!
DRIB-ul th'bawl!

Не трогай мяч руками.

Don't touch the ball with your hands.
Dohnt tuhch th'bawl with yor hanz.

Ударь мяч в ворота!

Kick the ball into the goal!
Kik th'bawl IN-too th'gohl!

/Следуй / Беги/ за мячом!

/Go/ Run/ after the ball!
/Goh/ Ruhn/ AF-ter th'bawl!

Забей гол!

Score a goal!
Skor uh gohl!

Ты забил/-а гол! Гол!

You have scored a goal! Goal!
Yoo hav skord uh gohl! Gohl!

Мо-лод-цы! Мо-лод-цы!

Way to go!
Wei t'goh!

Гола нет!

No goal!
Noh gohl!

Мяч был в воротах!

The ball was in the goal!
Th'bawl wuhz in th'gawl!

Передай (мне) мяч!

Pass the ball (to me)!
Pas th'bawl (t'mee)!

Мы проиграли!

We've lost!
Weev lawst!

В офсайде!

Off sides!
Awf sighdz!

СПОКОЙНЫЕ ИГРЫ — QUIET GAMES
KWIGH-et geimz

Поиграй в спокойную игру и отдохни.	Play a quiet game and rest. *Plei uh KWIGH-et geim and rest.*
Давай соберём пазл (вместе).	Let's do a puzzle (together). *Letz doo uh PUHZ-ul (tuh-GETH-er).*
Давай положим этот кусок здесь.	Let's put this (puzzle) piece in here. *Letz put this (PUHZ-ul) pees in heer.*
Ты думаешь, этот кусок сюда подходит?	Do you think this piece goes here? *Doo yoo think this pees gohz heer?*
Этот кусок не подходит.	This piece doesn't fit. *This pees DUHZ-ent fit.*
Какого куска не хватает?	Which piece is missing? *Wich pees iz MIS-'ng?*
Этот пазл слишком/ лёгкий/ трудный/!	This puzzle is too/ easy/ hard/! *This PUZ-ul iz too/ EE-zee/ hahrd/!*
Смотри в окно!	Look out the window! *Luk aout th'WIND-oh!*
Что ты видишь...	What do you see... *Waht doo yoo see...*
за деревом,	behind the tree, *bee-HIGHND th'tree,*
за мной,	behind me, *bee-HIGHND mee,*

Весело! _____

за матерью,	behind mommy, _bee-HIGHND MAHM-ee,_
под столом?	under the table? _UHN-der th'TEI-bl?_
Я ничего не вижу.	I don't see anything. _Igh dohnt see EN-ee-th'ng._
Давай сыграем в карты.	Let's play a game of cards. _Letz plei uh geim uhv kahrdz._
Ты можешь разобрать свою коллекцию марок.	You can sort your stamp collection. _Yoo kan sort yor stamp kuh-LEK-shuhn._

ПОЕЗДА И ГРУЗОВИКИ — TRAINS and TRUCKS
Treinz 'n truhks

Поезд отправляется!	All aboard! _Awl uh-BORD!_
Билеты, пожалуйста!	Tickets, please! _TIK-etz, pleez!_
Сколько стоит проезд?	What does the fare cost? _Waht duhz th'feir kawst?_
Я еду задним ходом.	I'm driving backwards. _Ighm DRIGHV-'ng BAK-werdz._
Я нагружаю свой грузовик.	I'm loading my truck. _Ighm LOHD-'ng migh truhk._
Ты доставляешь нефть в нефтевозе?	Are you delivering oil in your oil truck? _Ahr yoo dee-LIV-ring oyl in yor oyl truhk?_

Это не нефтевоз; это грузовик
для перевозки скота.

This is not an oil truck;
it's a cattle truck.
This iz naht an oyl truhk;
itz uh KAT-ul truhk.

Мне нравится джип.

I like the (4 x 4) pick-up.
Igh lighk th'(for bigh for) PIK-ahp.

Когда я получу водительские
права, я хочу...

When I have my license, I want...
Wen igh hav migh LIGH-sens,
igh wahnt...

Веселись!

Have fun! Enjoy yourself!
Hav fuhn! EN-joy yor-SELF!

The more the merrier!

Чем больше, тем лучше

В субботу днём | Saturday Afternoon

The opportunities for using English on Saturdays are unlimited. Saturdays were made for English! Chores to do using English, visits to friends using English, shopping, outings, sports. The list is endless as you can see.

Давайте/ сходим/ пойдём/ в кино/ в торговый центр/. | Let's go to the/ movies/ mall/.
Letz goh t'th'/MOOV-eez/ mawl/.

Могли бы........и ....пойти с нами? | May.....and ....come with us?
Mei ..... 'n........kuhm with us?

Что мы будем делать? | What shall we do?
Waht shal wee doo?

Давайте отправляться. | Let's get going. (Let's start.)
Letz get GOH-'ng. (Letz stahrt.)

Я бы лучше/ пошёл/ пошла/ на детскую площадку.	I'd rather go to the playground. *Ighd RATH-er goh t'th'PLEI-graound.*
Это (гораздо) веселее.	It's (much) more fun. *Itz muhch mor fuhn.*
Ну, пойдём(те)!	Let's go! (on foot) *Letz goh! (ahn fut)*
Ну, поедем(те)!	Let's go! (by vehicle) *Letz goh! (bigh VIH-ih-kul)*
Останься дома.	Stay home. *Stei hohm.*
Ты уже закончил/-а работу по дому?	Have you finished your chores? *Hav yoo FIN-isht yor chorz?*
После работы по дому ты можешь/ идти на улицу/ идти играть/.	After chores you can /go out/ go play/. *AF-ter chorz yoo kan/ goh aout/ goh plei/.*
Ты без дела (or) Тебе нечего делать?	Have you nothing to do? *Hav yoo NUHTH'ng t' doo?*
(Сейчас) мне нечего делать.	I have nothing to do (now). *Igh hav NUHTH-'ng t' doo (naou).*
Куда мне идти?	Where am I to go? *Wehr am igh t' goh?*
Мне некуда идти.	I have no where to go. *Igh hav noh wehr t'goh.*
Мне не с кем говорить.	I have no one to talk with. *Igh hav noh wuhn t'tawk with.*

В субботу днём_____

Есть школьная пьеса.	There is a school play. *Thehr iz uh skool plei.*
Есть кукольный спектакль в библиотеке.	There's a puppet show at the library. *Thehrz uh PUHP-et shoh at th'LIGH-brer-ee.*
Есть:	There is: *Thehr iz:*
выставка,	an exhibit, *an eg-ZIB-it,*
поездов,	train show, *trein shoh,*
садовых принадлежностей,	garden show, *GAHRD-en shoh,*
автомашин.	car show. *kahr shoh.*
Мы поедем на/ метро/ автобусе/.	We'll take the /subway/ bus/. *Weel teik th'/SUHB-wei/ buhs/.*
Нам можно поесть в ресторане?	Can we eat out? *Kan wee eet aout?*
Мне хочется есть в ресторане.	I want to eat in a restaurant. *Igh wahnt t'eet in uh REST-rahnt.*
Тебе нужно пойти к зубному врачу.	You have to go to the dentist. *Yoo hav t'goh t'th'DENT-ist.*
Хочешь, не хочешь, а идти надо.	You have to go whether you want to (go) or not. *Yoo hav t'goh WETH-er yoo wahnt too (t'goh) or naht.*

Нужно подогнать твои пластинки.	Your braces need to be adjusted. *Yor BREIS-ez need t'bee uh-JUHST-ed.*
Нет, тебе нельзя покрасить волосы в зелёный цвет!	No, you cannot dye your hair green! *Noh, yoo KAN-naht digh yor hehr green!*
Сядь в машину!	Get in the car! *Get in th'kahr!*
Мы поедем прокатиться на машине.	We'll go for a ride. *Weel goh for uh righd.*
Позвони...........и мы/ пойдём/ поедем/:	Call (up) ......and we'll go: *Kawl (ahp)..... and weel goh:*
кататься на роликовых досках,	skateboarding, *SKEIT-bord-'ng,*
кататься на роликах,	roller skating, *ROHL-er SKEIT-'ng,*
кататься на роликовых коньках.	roller blading. *ROHL-er BLEID-'ng.*
Давай послушаем мой новый компакт- диск.	Let's listen to my new CD! *Letz LIS-en t'migh noo see-DEE!*
Я бы лучше/ пошёл/ поехал/ на рыбалку.	I would rather go fishing. *Igh wud RATH-er goh FISH-'ng.*
У нас есть наживка и крючки.	We have the bait and hooks. *Wee hav th'beit and huks.*
Ты забыл/-а удочку.	You forgot the fishing rod. *Yoo for-GAHT th' FISH-'ng rahd.*

В субботу днём_____

| Ты хочешь пойти на рыбалку? | Would you like to go fishing? |
| | *Wud yoo lighk t'goh FISH-'ng?* |

| Я поймал/-а рыбу! | I caught a fish! |
| | *Igh kawt uh fish!* |

| Не могли бы мы закончить постройку дома на дереве? | Can't we finish building the tree house? |
| | *Kant wee FIN-ish BILD-'ng th'tree haous?* |

| Я принесу молоток, гвозди, пилу и доски. | I'll get the hammer, nails, saw and boards. |
| | *Ighl get th'HAM-er, neilz, saw and bordz.* |

| Давай (те) встретимся во дворе. | Let's meet in the back yard. |
| | *Letz meet in th'bak yahrd.* |

| Пойдём на чердак! | Let's go to the attic! |
| | *Letz goh t'th'AT-ik!* |

| Давай/ смотреть/ посмотрим/ футбол (по телевизору). | Let's watch soccer (on TV). |
| | *Letz wahch SAHK-er (ahn TEE-vee).* |

| Давай читать комиксы. | Let's read comic-books. |
| | *Letz reed KAHM-ik-buks.* |

| Пойдём/ на пляж/ на озеро/. | Let's go to the/ beach/ lake/. |
| | *Letz goh t'th'/beech/ leik/.* |

| Пойдём/ на море/ в бассейн/. | Let's go to the/ ocean/ pool/. |
| | *Letz goh t'th'/OH-shen/ pool/.* |

| Идём плавать. | Let's go swimming. |
| | *Letz goh SWIM-'ng.* |

| Идём кататься на водных лыжах. | Let's go waterskiing. |
| | *Letz goh WAWT-er-skee-'ng.* |

Я принесу полотенца,

I'll bring the towels,
Ighl bring th'taoulz.

пляжный зонтик и стул,

the beach umbrella/ chair,
th'beech uhm-BREL-uh/ chehr,

ведро и лопату.

the pail and shovel.
th'peil and SHUHV-el.

Вот мы и здесь!

Here we are!
Heer wee ahr!

Небо ясное.

The sky is clear.
Th'skigh iz kleer.

Расстели подстилку/ на солнце/ в тени/.

Spread the blanket in the/ sun/ shade/.
Spred th'BLANK-et in th'/sun/ sheid/.

Море/ бурное/ спокойное/.

The sea is/ rough/ calm/.
Th'see iz/ ruff/ kahm/.

Плавай здесь. Здесь мелко.

Swim here. It is shallow here.
Swim heer. It iz SHAL-oh heer.

Мы можем делиться друг с другом,

We can share,
Wee kan shehr,

по очереди пользоваться,

take turns using,
teik ternz YOOZ-'ng,

надувным матрасом.

the air mattress.
th'ehr MAT-tres.

/ Выходи/ Выйди/ из воды.

Come out of the water.
Kuhm aout uhv th'WAWT-er.

Ты только что поел/-а!

You have just eaten!
Yoo hav juhst EET-en!

115

В субботу днём

Тебе нельзя идти обратно в воду.

You are not allowed back in the water.
Yoo ahr naht uh-laoud bak in th'WAWT-er.

Тебе слишком холодно.

You're too cold.
Yor too kohld.

Ты дрожишь от холода.

You're shivering with cold.
Yor SHIV-ring with kohld.

Не простудись.

Don't catch cold.
Dohnt kach kohld.

Здесь есть медузы!

There are jelly fish here!
Thehr ahr JEL-ee fish heer!

Ну, уже поздно.

It's getting late.
Itz GET-'ng leit.

Почему бы нам не:

Why don't we:
Wigh dohnt wee:

поискать ракушки,

look for little seashells,
luk for LIT-ul SEE-shelz,

построить замок из песка,

build a sand castle,
bild uh sand KAS-ul,

понаблюдать за птицами?

watch the birds?
wahch th'birdz?

Ты хочешь лечь (на подстилку) ?

Do you want to lie down (on the blanket)?
Doo yoo wahnt t'ligh daoun (ahn th'BLANK-et)?

Смотри за/ сестрой/ братом/.

Watch your/ sister/ brother/.
Wahch yor /SIS-ter/ BRUTH-er/.

Я останусь здесь и буду /за ним/ за ней/ смотреть.	I'll stay here and watch/ him/ her/. *Ighl stei heer 'n wahch/ him/ her/.*
Ты хочешь загореть?	Do you want to get a tan? *Doo yoo wahnt t'get uh tan?*
Ты сгорел/-а (на солнце).	You got sunburnt. *Yoo gaht SUN-bernt.*
Где крем?	Where is the lotion? *Wehr iz th'LOHSH-uhn?*
Где очки от солнце?	Where are the sunglasses? *Wehr ahr th'SUHN-glas-ez?*
Какой прекрасный день для/ купания/ катания на лыжах/!	What a beautiful day for/ swimming/ skiing/! *Waht uh BYOO-tih-ful dei for/ SWIM-'ng/ SKEE-'ng/!*
Нам не нужно брать в аренду:	We don't need to rent: *Wee dohnt need t'rent:*
лыжи,	skis, *skeez,*
лыжные палки,	ski poles, *skee pohlz,*
лыжные ботинки.	ski boots. *skee bootz.*
У нас есть своё снаряжение.	We have our own equipment. *Wee hav aour ohn ee-KWIP-ment.*
Моё снаряжение нужно подогнать.	My equipment needs to be adjusted. *Migh ee-KWIP-ment needz t'bee uh-JUHST-ed.*

В субботу днём

Снег слишком/ мягий/ твёрдый/.

The snow is too/ soft/ hard/.
Th'snoh iz too/sawft/ hahrd/.

Сколько стоит билет на канатный подъёмник?

How much is a chairlift ticket?
Haou muhch iz uh CHEHR-lift TIK-et?

Где билетная касса?

Where is the ticket office?
Wehr iz th'TIK-et AWF-is?

Не иди на самый верх горы!

Don't go to the top of the mountain!
Dohnt goh t'th'tahp uhv th'MAOUN-ten!

Горка слишком крутая!

The hill is too steep!
Th' hil iz too steep!

Это опасно! Не так быстро!

That's dangerous!
Thatz DANJ-er-uhs!

Туда опасно идти.

It's dangerous to go there.
Itz DANJ-er-uhs t'goh thehr.

Какой форм!

What form!
Waht form!

Тебе холодно?

Are you cold?
Ahr yoo kohld?

Мне/ холодно/ жарко/ тепло/.

I am/ cold/ hot/ warm/.
Igh am/kohld/ haht/ wawrm/.

Ты устал/-а?

Are you tired?
Ahr yoo TIGHR-ed?

Хорошо бы сейчас выпить чего--нибудь/ горячего/ тёплого/.

It would be nice to have something/ hot/ warm/ to drink.
It wud bee nighs t'hav SUHM-th'ng / haht/ wawrm/ t'drink.

Давайте зайдём вовнутрь –

Let's go inside –
Letz goh in-SIGHD –

   чтобы отдохнуть,

   to rest,
   t'rest,

   чтобы поесть,

   to eat,
   t'eet,

   чтобы согреться.

   to warm up.
   t'wawrm ahp.

Когда мы/ уходим/ уезжаем/?

When are we leaving?
Wen ahr wee LEEV-ng?

Пора идти домой.

It is time to go home.
It iz tighm t'goh hohm.

Упаковывай свои вещи.

Pack up your things.
Pak ahp yor thn'gz.

Я уже/ готов/ готова/:

I'm ready:
Ighm RED-ee:

   идти,

   to go,
   t'goh,

   идти гулять,

   to go for a walk,
   t'goh for uh wawk,

   есть.

   to eat.
   t'eet.

Ну, уж если идти, так сейчас.

Well, if we're going, let's
go now.
*Wel, if weer GOH-'ng, letz
goh naou.*

Будет сильное движение.

There will be a lot of traffic.
Thehr wil bee uh laht uv TRAF-ik.

В субботу днём

Смотри, чтобы у тебя всё (с собой) было.	Make sure that you have everything (with you). *Meik shoor that yoo hav EV-ree-th'ng (with you.)*
Тебе было весело?	Did you have a good time? *Did yoo hav uh gud tighm?*
Мне было весело.	I had a good time. *Igh had uh gud tighm.*
Мне весело.	I'm having a good time. *Ighm HAV-'ng uh gud tighm.*

Out of Sight, Out of Mind!

С глаз долой, из сердца вон!

Восклицания

Ой!

Ну что же?!

Оп-пля!

Нет проблем!

Хорошо! Всё в порядке!

Давай!

Exclamations

Ouch! Oops! Ow!
Aouch! Oops! Aou!

What?!
Waht?!

Up/ down/ you go!
Ahp/ daoun/ yoo goh!

No problem!
Noh PRAH-blem!

All right! Okay!
Awl right! Oh-KEI!

Go ahead! (permission)
Goh uh-hed! (per-MISH-uhn)

Восклицания

Здорово! Прекрасно!	Great! *Greit!*
Вот это дело!	Now you're talking! *Naou yor TAWK-'ng!*
Как глупо!	How silly! *Haou SIL-ee!*
Тебе/ радостно/ весело/?	Are you/ sad/ happy/? *Ahr yoo/ sad/ HAP-ee/?*
Мы рады, что ты победил/-а.	We're glad that you won. *Weer glad that yoo wuhn.*
Помоги(те)!	Help! *Help!*
Не рискуй!	Don't take risks! *Dohnt teik risks!*
Я буду/ осторожен/ остарожна/.	I'll be careful. *Ighl bee KEHR-ful.*
Кто виноват?	Whose fault is it? *Hooz fawlt iz it?*
Мне жаль. Это моя вина.	I'm sorry. It's my fault. *Ighm SAHR-ee. Itz migh fawlt.*
Тут ничего не сделаешь.	It can't be helped. *It kant bee helpt.*
Я ничего не могу поделать!	I can't help it! *I kant help it!*
Ничего не помогает!	Nothing's helping! *NUHTH-'ngz HELP-'ng!*

Я сдаюсь!

I give up!
Igh giv ahp!

Вот как!

Is that so!
Iz that soh!

Это не так!

That's not so!
Thatz naht soh!

Безусловно это так!

It certainly is!
It SERT-en-lee iz!

Как хочешь!

As you wish!
Az yoo wish!

Прежде всего...

First of all...
Ferst uhv awl...

Почему так долго?

Why is it taking so long?
Wigh iz it TEIK- 'ng soh lawng?

Нет, вы видали такое!

Well, what do you know!
(Expressing surprise!)
Wel, waht doo yoo noh!

Какая очередь!

What a line!
Waht uh lighn!

Вот как?

Really?
REEL-ee?

Я верю тебе.

I believe you.
Igh bee-LEEV yoo.

Можешь надеяться на меня.

You can count on me.
Yoo kan kaount ahn mee.

Ничего страшного.

It's no big deal.
Itz noh big deel.

Восклицания

Делай, как хочешь.	Do as you like. *Doo az yoo lighk.*
Мне всё равно!	I don't care! *Igh dohnt kehr!*
Отдыхай! (or) Отдохни!	Relax! *Ree-LAKS!*
Будь/ разумен/ разумна/.	Be reasonable. *Bee REE-zuhn-uh-bl.*
Почему ты отказываешься/ играть/ говорить/?	Why do you refuse/ to play/ to speak/? *Wigh doo yoo ree-FYOOZ/ t'plei/ t'speek/?*
Пусть будет по-твоему.	Have it your way. *Hav it yor wei.*
Ты меня не понимаешь.	You don't understand me. *Yoo dohnt uhn-der-STAND mee.*
Мне всё равно.	It's all the same to me. *Itz awl th'seim t'mee.*
Давай покончим с этим.	Let's get this over with. *Letz get this OH-ver with.*
Это не твоё дело.	That doesn't concern you. *That DUHZ-ent kuhn-SERN yoo.*
С каких пор?	Since when? *Sins wen?*
Я это тебе сто раз говорил/-а.	I've told you a hundred times. *Ighv tohld yoo uh HUHN-dred tighmz.*
Откуда мне знать?	How should I know? *Haou shud igh noh?*

Кто знает?

Who knows?
Hoo nohz?

Это (не) важно.

That's (not) important.
Thatz (naht) im-PORT-ent.

Конечно! Конечно нет!

Of course! Of course not!
Uhv kors! Uhv kors naht!

Это уж слишком.

That's going too far.
Thatz GOH-'ng too fahr.

Ни в коем случае! (or) Ни за что!

No way!
Noh wei!

Это правда или ты всё это
придумал/-а?

Is that true or did you make up
that story?
*Iz that troo or did yoo meik ahp
that STAWR-ee?*

Правильно!

Correct!
Kuhr-REKT!

Безусловно!

Sure!
Shoor!

Всё равно дела не поправишь.

There's nothing you can do
about it.
*Thehrz NUHTH-'ng yoo kan
doo uh-BAOUT it.*

Тем лучше.

So much the better.
Soh muhch th'BET-er.

Всё к лучшему.

It's all for the best.
Itz awl for th'best.

Я точно не знаю.

I'm not certain.
Ighm naht SERT-en.

Восклицания

Я/ согласен/ согласна/ (с тобой).	I agree (with you). *Igh uh-GREE (with yoo).*
Я тоже.	So do I. *Soh doo igh.*
Это очень интересно.	It's very interesting. *Itz VER-ee IN-trest'ng.*
Ты очень смешной мальчик!	You're a very funny boy! *Yor uh VER-ee FUHN-ee boy!*
Ты очень смешная девочка!	You're a very funny girl! *Yor uh VER-ee FUHN-ee girl!*
Как смешно! Это не смешно!	How funny! That is not funny! *Haou FUHN-ee! That iz naht FUHN-ee!*
Вздор!	Nonsense! *NAHN-sens!*
Везёт! Не везёт!	In luck! Out of luck! *In luhk! Aout uhv luhk!*
Тебе везёт! Тебе повезло!	Lucky you! *LUHK-ee yoo!*
Как ужасно!	How awful! *Haou AW-ful!*
Очень жаль.	That's too bad. *Thatz too bad.*
Как жаль!	What a pity! *Waht uh PIT-ee!*
Это невероятно!	That is unbelievable! *That iz un-bee-LEEV-uh-bl!*

Замечательно!	Wonderful! Marvelous! *WUHN-der-ful! MAHRV-el-uhs!*
Очень хорошо. Отлично.	Very good. Excellent. *VER-ee gud. EK-sul-ent.*
Это ты так только пошутил/-а?	You were just joking, weren't you? *Yoo wer juhst JOHK'ng, WER-ent yoo?*
Не шути.	Don't joke. *Dohnt johk.*
Я спрашиваю серьёзно.	I'm asking seriously. *Ighm ASK-'ng yoo SEER-ee-us-lee.*
Надеюсь, что/ да/ нет/!	I hope/ so/ not/! *Igh hohp/ soh/ naht/!*
Я думаю, что/ да/ нет/!	I think /so/ not/! *Igh think/ soh/ naht/!*
Как бы не так!	I should say not! *Igh shud sei naht!*
А-а, понятно!	Oh, I see! *Oh, igh see!*
Это ясно?	Is that clear? *Iz that kleer?*
Не беспокойся! (or) Не волнуйся!	Don't worry! *Dohnt WER-ee!*
Всякое /бывает/ случается!	Accidents happen! *AK-sid-ents HAP-en!*
Не бойся (собаку).	Don't be afraid (of the dog). *Dohnt bee uh-FREID (uhv th'dawg).*

Восклицания

Успокойся!	Calm down! *Kahm daoun!*
Ради Бога!	For heaven's sake! *For HEV-enz seik!*
Не сердись	Don't be angry. *Dohnt bee ANG-ree.*
Ну, ничего, ничего...	There, there... *Thehr, thehr...*
Всё будет нормально.	Everything will be all right. *EV-ree-th'ng wil bee awl right.*
Если я могу это сделать, то и ты сможешь.	If I can do it, then you can do it. *If igh kan doo it, then yoo kan doo it.*
Это (не) правильно.	It's (not) /right/ just/ fair/. *Itz (naht) /right/ juhst/ fehr/.*
Это не обязательно.	That's not necessary. *Thatz naht NES-es-ehr-ee.*
Не вздумай!	You'd better not! *Yood BET-er naht!*
Убери руки!	Hands off! *Hanz awf!*
Ну и беспорядок!	What a mess! *Waht uh mes!*
Довольно! (or) Хватит!	Enough of that! *Ee-NUFF uhv that!*
Мне надоело!	I'm fed up! *Ighm fed ahp!*

Что мне делать?

What am I to do?
Waht am igh too doo?

Не мешай мне.

Don't disturb me.
Dohnt dis-TERB mee.

У меня не было ни одной
свободной минуты!

I haven't had a moment to myself!
*Igh HAV-ent had uh MOH-ment
t'migh-SELF!*

Что надо сделать?

What's to be done?
Wahts t'bee duhn?

В чём дело?

What's the matter?
Wahts th'MAT-er?

Это правда, не так ли?

That's true, don't you think?
Thatz troo, dohnt yoo think?

Ты знаешь, ...

You know, ...
Yoo noh...

Ну конечно!

Yes, indeed!
Yes, in-DEED!

Не может быть! Неужели?

You don't say! Really?
Yoo dohnt sei! REEL-ee?

Как обычно.

As usual.
Az YOOZH-ih-wel.

Будь здоров/-a!

Bless you!
Bles yoo!

Что такое?

What's wrong?
Wahts rawng?

Ничего.

Never mind.
NEV-er mighnd.

Я был/-а неправ/-а.

I was wrong.
Igh wuhz rawng.

Почему ты жалуешься?

Why are you complaining?
Wigh ahr yoo kuhm-PLEIN-'ng?

Осторожно!

Look out! Watch out!
Luk aout! Wahch aout!

Сейчас же!

Right now!
Right naou!

Опасно! Осторожно!

Danger! Caution!
DEINJ-er! KAWSH-uhn!

Господи! Боже мой!

Goodness gracious!
GUD-nes GREISH-uhs!

Это дело нешуточное!

This is no laughing matter!
This iz noh LAF-'ng MAT-er!

Над чем ты смеёшься?

What are you laughing at?
Waht ahr yoo LAF-'ng at?

Не смейся.

Don't laugh.
Dohnt laf.

Так тебе и надо!

It serves you right!
It servz yoo right!

Тебе нельзя так говорить!

You must not say that!
Yoo muhst naht sei that!

Господи! О Боже!

My God! Oh, God!
Migh gahd, Oh, Gahd!

Это очень большой!

It's immense!
Itz ee-MENS!

Хорошо. Можно.

That's fine.
Thatz fighn.

Дело в шляпе!

It's in the bag!
Its in th'bag!

Я тоже! (or) И я!

Me too!
Mee too!

Что ты хочешь этим сказать?

What do you mean by this?
Waht doo yoo meen bigh this?

Что ты пытаешься сказать?

What are you trying to say?
Waht ahr yoo TRIGH-'ng too sei?

Скажи то, что думаешь.

Say what you think.
Sei waht yoo think.

Это всё! (or) Больше нет!

That's all! All gone!
Thatz awl! Awl gahn!

Вот и всё!

It's over! That's all!
Itz OH-ver! Thatz awl!

... во что бы то ни стало!

...no matter what happens!
...noh MAT-er waht HAP-enz!

Not the gift is dear, love is dear.

Не дорог подарок, дорога любовь

Празднование дня рождения

Birthday Party

С днём рождения!
Это для тебя. (or) Это тебе.

Happy Birthday! This is for you.
HAP-ee BIRTH-dei! This iz for yoo.

Какой подарок ты хочешь на день рождения?

What kind of present would
you like for your birthday?
*Waht kighnd uv PREZ-ent wud
yoo lighk for yor BIRTH-dei?*

Тебе бы хотелось устроить вечеринку на день своего рождения?

Would you like to have a
birthday party?
*Wud yoo lighk t'hav uh
BIRTH-dei PAHR-tee?*

Мы будем отмечать твой день рождения в субботу.

We'll celebrate your
birthday on Saturday.
*Weel SEL-uh-breit yor
BIRTH-dei ahn SAT-er-dei.*

Мы пригласим твоих друзей.	We'll invite your friends. *Weel in-VIGHT yor frendz.*
Мы можем пригласить всех моих друзей?	Can we invite all my friends? *Kan wee in-VIGHT awl migh frendz?*
Может быть мы устроим пикник!	Maybe we could have a picnic! *MEI-bee wee kud hav uh PIK-nik!*
У нас будут:	We'll have: *Weel hav:*
трубочки с мороженым,	ice cream cones, *ighs kreem kohnz,*
воздушные шары, шляпы,	balloons, hats, *buh-LOONZ, hatz,*
игры, подарки.	games, presents. *geimz, PREZ-ents.*
У нас будет торт.	We'll have cake. *Weel hav keik.*
Где ты хочешь устроить вечеринку?	Where do you want to have the party? *Wehr doo yoo wahnt t'hav th'PAHR-tee?*
дома, в парке,	at home, in the park, *at hohm, in th'pahrk,*
в ресторане, на пляже?	in a restaurant or at the beach? *in uh REST-rahnt or at th'beech?*
Я купил/-а тебе открытку и подарок.	I bought you a card and a present. *Igh bawht yoo uh kahrd 'nd uh PREZ-ent.*

Празднование дня рождения_____

Сколько тебе лет? Я не знаю.	How old are you? I don't know. *Haou ohld ahr yoo? Igh dohnt noh.*
Мне/ пять/ десять/ лет.	I am/ five/ ten/ years old. *Igh am/ fighv/ ten/ yeerz ohld.*
Когда твой день рождения?	When is your birthday? *Wen iz yor BIRTH-dei?*
Мой день рождения десятого мая.	My birthday is on May 10. *Migh BIRTH-dei iz ahn mei tenth.*
Чего бы тебе хотелось больше всего?	What do you wish the most? *Waht doo yoo wish th'mohst?*
Кем ты будешь? (когда вырастешь)	What will you be? (when you grow up) *Waht wil yoo bee? (Wen yoo groh ahp)*
Кем ты хочешь стать, когда вырастешь?	What do you want to be when you grow up? *Waht doo yoo wahnt too bee wen yoo groh ahp?*
Я буду учителем, пожарным.	I will be a teacher, fireman. *Igh wil bee uh TEECH-er, FIGHR-m'n.*
Я буду/ богатым/ богатой/.	I will be rich. *Igh wil bee rich.*
Сколько свечек?	How many candles? *Haou MEN-ee KAND-ulz?*
Давайте их сосчитаем!	Let's count them! *Letz kaount them!*
Задуй свечки!	Blow out the candles! *Bloh aout th'KAND-ulz!*

134

Порежь торт!

Cut the cake!
Kuht th'keik!

Подели торт на шесть кусков.

Divide the cake into six pieces.
D'VIGHD th' keik IN-too siks
PEES-ez.

Я хотел/-а бы:

I'd like:
IGHD lighk:

шоколадного мороженого,

(some) chocolate ice cream,
(suhm) CHAWK-let ighs kreem,

персикового мороженого,

(some) peach ice cream,
(suhm) peech ighs kreem,

ванильного мороженого.

(some) vanilla ice cream.
(suhm) vah-NEL-uh ighs kreem.

Что ты получил/-а в подарок?

What did you receive for a
present?
Waht did yoo ree-SEEV for uh
PREZ-ent?

Все дарят имениннику много
подарков.

Everyone gives a lot of presents
to the birthday person.
EV-ree-wuhn givz uh laht uhv
PREZ-ents t'th'BIRTH-dei
PER-suhn.

Спасибо за подарок.

Thanks for the gift.
Thanks for th'gift.

Какая замечательная вечеринка!

What a great party!
Waht uh greit PAHR-tee!

Теперь мне можно получить
водительские права?

Now can I get my driver's
license?
Naou kan igh get migh
DRIGHV-erz LIGH-sens?

135

sleep is better than medicine.

Сон лучше всякого лекарства

Пора спать	Bedtime

This is a good time to read a story in English to your child. The language he hears before going to sleep will linger in his mind during the night. This might also be a golden opportunity to learn and recite prayers in English.

Какой зевок!	What a yawn! *Waht uh yawn!*
Ты зеваешь.	You're yawning. *Yor YAWN- 'ng.*
Ты/ устал/-а?	Are you tired? *Ahr yoo TIGHR-ed?*
Ты хочешь спать?	Are you drowsy ? *Ahr yoo DRAOUZ-ee?*
(Тебе) пора спать.	Time (for you) to go to bed. *Tighm (for yoo) t'goh t'bed.*
Ты/ должен/должна/идти спать.	You should go to bed. *Yoo shud goh t'bed.*

Ещё рано!

It's still early!
Itz stil ERL-ee!

Не ложись сегодня поздно спать.

Don't stay up late tonight.
Dohnt stei ahp leit tuh-NIGHT.

Я уложу тебя спать.

I'm putting you to bed.
Ighm PUT- 'ng yoo t'bed.

Мне уже надо идти спать?

Do I have to go to bed already?
Doo igh hav t'goh t'bed
awl- RED-ee?

Иди и принеси (свою) книгу.

Go get your book.
Goh get yor buk.

Расскажи мне рассказ.

Tell me a story.
Tel mee uh STAWR-ee.

Я прочитаю тебе рассказ,

I'll read you a story,
Ighl reed yoo uh STAWR-ee,

...перед тем как ты пойдёшь спать.

...before you go to bed.
...bee-FOR yoo goh t'bed.

Однажды...(or) Давным-давно...

Once upon a time....
Wuhns uh-PAHN uh tighm...

Ты смотришь телевизор?

Are you watching TV?
Ahr yoo WAHCH- 'ng tee-vee?

Сними/ одежду/ обувь/.

Take off your/ clothes/ shoes/.
Teik awf yor/ klohz/ shooz/.

Надень пижаму.

Put on your pajamas.
Put ahn yor pah-JAH-mahz.

Пора спать

Повесь свою рубашку.	Hang up your shirt. *Hang ahp yor shert.*
Подбери свою одежду!	Pick up your clothes! *Pik ahp yor klohz!*
Эти носки нужно выстирать.	These socks need to be washed. *Theez sahks need t'bee wahsht.*
Ты готов/-а идти спать?	Are you ready for bed? *Ahr yoo RED-ee for bed?*
Приготовься.	Get ready. *Get RED-ee.*
Я уже/ готов/ готова/.	I'm ready. *Ighm RED-ee.*
Пожелай папе,,Спокойной ночи."	Say, "Good Night" to Daddy. *Sei, "Gud Night" t'DAD-ee.*
Ты/ произнёс/ произнесла/ молитву?	Did you say your prayers? *Did yoo sei yor prehrz?*
Ты становишься тяжёлым/ой!	You're getting heavy! *Yor GET-'ng HEV-ee!*
Закрой глаза.	Close your eyes. *Klohz yor ighz.*
Ложись. Ляг.	Lie down. *Ligh daoun.*
Тише, пожалуйста.	Quiet, please. *KWIGH-et, pleez.*
Тебе нужно/ лежать в постели/ спать/.	You must/stay in bed/ sleep/. *Yoo muhst/ stei in bed/ sleep/.*

Я тебя накрою.

I'll cover you up.
Ighl KUHV-er yoo ahp.

Ты ещё не в кровати?

You're not in bed yet?
Yor naht in bed yet?

Сейчас не слишком рано идти спать!

It's not too early to go to bed now!
Itz naht too ERL-ee t'goh t'bed naou!

Ты хочешь, чтобы свет был включён?

Do you want the light lit?
Doo yoo wahnt th'light lit?

Мама тебя любит!

Mommy loves you!
MAHM-ee luhvz yoo!

Ты мокрый/ мокрая?

Are you wet?
Ahr yoo wet?

У тебя режутся зубы.

You're teething.
Yor TEETH-th'ng.

Ты/ проснулся/ проснулась?

Did you wake up?
Did yoo weik ahp?

Ты не спишь?

Are you awake?
Ahr yoo uh-WEIK?

Ты спишь?

Are you asleep?
Ahr yoo uh-SLEEP?

Почему ты не ещё спишь?

Why aren't you asleep yet?
Wigh AHR-ent yoo uh-SLEEP yet?

Я хочу ещё поспать.

I want to sleep a little longer.
Igh wahnt t'sleep uh LIT-ul LAWNG-er.

Пора спать

Тебе не спится?	Can't you sleep? *Kant yoo sleep?*
Не разбуди/ его/ её/!	Don't awaken/ him/ her/! *Dohnt uh-WEIK-en/ him/ her/!*
Чего ты хочешь,/ мой малыш/ моя малышка/?	What do you want, my little one? *Waht doo yoo wahnt, migh LIT-ul wuhn?*
У тебя царапина на колене.	You have a scratch on your knee. *Yoo hav uh skrach ahn yor nee.*
Ты нездоров/-а?	Aren't you well? *AHR-ent yoo wel?*
У тебя болит/ живот/ животик/?	Do you have a/ stomach/ tummy/ ache? *Doo yoo hav uh/ STUHM-ik/ TUHM-ee/ aik?*
От чего тебе стало нехорошо?	What made you sick? *Waht meid yoo sik?*
У тебя кружится голова?	Do you feel dizzy? *Doo yoo feel DIZ-ee?*
Голова кружится.	I'm dizzy. *Ighm DIZ-ee.*
У тебя температура?	Do you have a fever? *Doo yoo hav uh FEEV-er?*
У тебя болит/ голова/ зуб/?	Do you have a/ headache/ toothache/? *Doo yoo hav uh/ HED-aik/ TOOTH-aik/?*

У меня (сильно) болит голова.

I have a (bad) headache.
Igh hav uh (bad) HED-aik.

Не тряси головой.

Don't shake your head.
Dohnt sheik yor hed.

У меня болят зубы.

My teeth hurt.
Migh teeth hert.

У тебя (есть) сыпь.

You have a rash.
Yoo hav uh rash.

У тебя опухли железы.

Your glands are swollen.
Yor glanz ahr SWOHL-en.

Высуни язык!

Stick out your tongue!
Stik aout yor tuhng!

Покажи язык.

Show your tongue
Shoh yor tuhng.

У тебя начинается грипп.

You're getting the flu.
Yor GET'ng th'floo.

/Я/ Ты/ простудился/
простудилась/.

/ I/ You/ have caught a cold.
/Igh/ Yoo/ hav kawt uh kohld.

Ты/ кашляешь/ чихаешь/.

You're/ coughing/ sneezing/.
Yor/ KAWF-'ng/ SNEEZ-'ng/.

У тебя болит горло?

Do you have a sore throat?
Doo yoo hav uh sor throht?

Я измерю тебе температуру.

I'll take your temperature.
Ighl teik yor TEMP-per-chur.

У тебя/ жар/ кашель/.

You have a/ fever/ cough/.
Yoo hav uh/ FEEV-er/ kawf/.

Тебе необходимо как следует
отдохнуть.

You have to get a good rest.
Yoo hav t'get uh gud rest.

Тебе нужно что-то от кашля.	You need something for the cough. *Yoo need SUHM-th'ng for th'kawf.*
Тебе нужно принимать лекарство (от кашля).	You have to take your (cough) medicine. *Yoo hav t'teik yor (kawf) MED-ih-sin.*
Завтра тебе нужно оставаться в постели.	Tomorrow you'll have to stay in bed. *Tuh-MAHR-oh yool hav t'stei in bed.*
У тебя что-нибудь болит?	Does something hurt? *Duhz SUHM-th'ng hert?*
У тебя болит/ рука/ нога/?	Does your/ arm/ foot/ hurt? *Duhz yor/ ahrm/ fut/ hert?*
Ты уколол/-а палец?	Did you prick your finger? *Did yoo prik yor FEENG-er?*
Ты хочешь пластырь?	Do you want a bandaid? *Doo yoo wahnt uh BAND-eid?*
Ты хорошо спал/-а?	Did you sleep well? *Did yoo sleep wel?*
(Почему) ты плохо себя чувствуешь?	(Why) do you feel bad? *(Wigh) doo yoo feel bad?*
Ты хорошо себя чувствуешь?	Do you feel good? *Doo yoo feel gud?*
Когда я буду лучше себя чувствовать?	When will I feel better? *Wen wil igh feel BET-er?*
Тебе скоро будет лучше.	You'll feel better soon. *Yool feel BET-er soon.*

142

Выздоравливай!

Get better!
Get BET-er!

Можно мне переночевать у
(..........) ?

May I sleep at (name)'s house?
Mei igh sleep at (.........) haous?

Можно (name) у нас переночевать?

May (name) sleep over at our house?
Mei (neim) sleep OH-ver at aour haous?

Произнеси молитву.

Say your prayers.
Sei yor *prehrz.*

Тебе удобно?

Are you comfortable?
Ahr yoo KUHMF-ter-bl?

Спи спокойно!

Sleep well!
Sleep wel!

Тссс!

Shhh!
Shhh!

Приятных сновидений!

Sweet dreams!
Sweet dreemz!

Morning gray -- a pretty day.

Серенькое утро, красненький денёк

Погода   ## The Weather

Try sharing a picture book about weather with your child and discuss the pictures using English. This could be more of a school kind of chapter if you and your child want to play school. Flash cards to make, maps to draw, temperatures to record, fun to be had!

Как красиво!

How beautiful!
Haou BYOO-tih-ful!

Какой чудесный день!

What a lovely day!
Waht uh LUHV-lee dei!

Облаков нет.

There are no clouds.
Thehr ahr noh klaoudz.

Солнечно.

It is sunny.
It iz SUHN-ee.

144

Солнце светит.

The sun's shining.
Th'suhnz SHIGHN-'ng.

Сегодня пасмурно.

It's overcast today.
Itz OH-ver-kast tuh-DEI.

Сегодня (очень) жарко.

It's (very) hot today.
Itz (VER-ee) haht tuh-DEI.

Тепло. Лето.

It's warm. It's summer.
Itz wahrm. Itz SUHM-er.

У нас период сильной жары.

We're having a heat wave.
Weer HAV-'ng uh heet weiv.

Нет ни мапейшего ветерка.

There's not a bit of wind.
Thehrz naht uh bit uhv wind.

Я потею.

I'm sweating.
Ighm SWET-'ng.

/Ветрено./ Облачно/.

It's/ windy/ cloudy/.
Itz/ WIND-ee/ KLAOUD-ee/.

(Слегка) прохладно.
Холодновато.

It's (a bit) cool. It's a bit cold.
Itz (uh bit) kool. Itz uh bit kohld.

Становится сыро.

It's getting damp.
Itz GET-'ng damp.

Тебе нужна куртка./ Тебе нужен свитер.

You need a/ jacket/ sweater/.
Yoo need uh/ JAK-et/ SWET-er/.

(Опять) идёт дождь.

It's raining (again).
Itz REIN-'ng (uh-GEN).

Посмотри на/ дождь/ снег/.

Look at the/ rain/ snow/.
Luk at th'/ rein/ snoh/.

На улице лужи.

There are puddles in the street.
Thehr ahr PUHD-lz in th'street.

У тебя мокрые туфли.

Your shoes are wet.
Yor shooz ahr wet.

Какая сегодня ужасная погода!

What awful weather today!
Waht AW-ful WETH-er tuh-DEI!

Это ливень.

It's a shower.
Itz uh SHAOU-er.

Сегодня высокая влажность.

The humidity is high today.
*Th'hyoo-MID-ih-tee iz high
tuh-DEI.*

Скоро будет светло.

It will be light soon.
It wil bee light soon.

Небо/ тёмное/ серое/.

The sky is/ dark/ gray/.
Th'skigh iz/ dahrk/ grei/.

Скоро будет темно.

It will soon be dark.
It wil soon bee dahrk.

/Гремит гром. /Сверкает
молния/.

It's/ thundering/ lightening/.
*Itz/ THUHND-er-'ng/
LIGHT-n'ng/.*

Идёт град.

It's hailing.
Itz HEIL-'ng.

Какая гроза!

What a storm!
Waht uh storm!

Какой туман!

What fog!
Waht fahg!

Стоит туман.

It's foggy.
Itz FAHG-ee.

Подожди, пока не пройдёт
дождь.

Wait until the rain stops.
Weit un-TIL th'rein stahps.

Ты видишь радугу?

Do you see the rainbow?
Doo yoo see th'REIN-boh?

Начинает идти снег!

It's beginning to snow!
Itz bee-GIN-'ng t'snoh!

Идёт снег.

It's snowing.
Itz SNOH-'ng.

Похоже, идёт/ дождь/ снег/.

It looks like it's/ raining/
snowing/.
*It luks lighk itz/ REIN-'ng/
SNOH-'ng.*

Снежинки падают!

Snowflakes are falling!
SNOH-fleiks ahr FAWL-ng!

Погода (совсем) как зимой!

It's (really) wintry weather!
Itz (REEL-ee) WIN-tree WETH-er!

Как сверкает снег!

How the snow sparkles!
Haou th'snoh SPAHRK-ulz!

Может быть, мы сможем слепить
снеговика.

Perhaps we can build a
snowman.
*Per-HAPS wee kan bild uh
SNOH-man.*

/Дождь/ снег/ перестал.

The/ rain/ snow/ has stopped.
Th'/ rein/ snoh/ haz stahpt.

Снег тает.

The snow is melting.
Th'snoh iz MELT-'ng.

Better late than never.

Лучше поздно, чем никогда

Время

Который час?

Сколько времени...?

Сейчас час.

Сейчас/ два/ три/ четыре/ часа.

Сейчас/ пять/ шесть/ семь/ часов.

Сейчас четверть четвёртого.

Time

What time is it?
Waht tighm iz it?

How much time...?
Haou muhch tighm...?

It is one o'clock.
It iz wuhn oh-KLAHK.

It is / two/ three/ four/ o'clock.
It iz/ too/ three/ for/ oh-KLAHK.

It is/ five/ six/ seven/ o'clock.
*It iz/ fighv/ siks/ SEV-en/
oh-KLAHK.*

It is quarter after three.
It iz KWAWT-er AF-ter three.

Сейчас двадцать минут седьмого.

It is six twenty.
It iz siks TWENT-ee.

Сейчас без четверти семь.

It is quarter of seven.
It iz KWAWT-er uhv SEV-en.

Сейчас без двадцати семь.

It is twenty to seven.
It iz TWENT-ee too SEV-en.

Сейчас восемь часов.

It is eight o'clock.
It iz eit oh-KLAHK.

Сейчас девять часов.

It is nine o'clock.
It iz nighn oh-KLAHK

Сейчас половина десятого.

It is nine thirty.
It iz nighn THIRT-ee.

Сейчас десять минут
одиннадцатого.

It is ten after ten (o'clock).
It iz ten AF-ter ten.

Сейчас одиннадцать часов.

It is eleven o'clock.
It iz ee-LEV-en oh-KLAHK.

Сейчас половина первого.

It is twelve thirty.
It is twelv THIRT-ee.

Сейчас/ ночь/ полночь/.

It is/ night/ midnight/.
It iz/ night/ MID-night/.

Сейчас/ день/ полдень/.

It is/ day/ noon/.
It iz/ dei/ noon/.

Сейчас/ утро/ вторая половина
дня/ вечер/.

It's/ morning/ afternoon/
evening/.
*Itz/ MORN-'ng/ AF-ter-noon/
EEV-'ng.*

Рано/ Поздно/.

It is/ early/ late/.
It iz/ ERL-ee/ leit/.

Время_____

Длится/ давно/ недавно/.	It lasts a/ long/ short/ time.
	It lasts uh /lawng/ short/ tighm.
Как можно/ скорей/ скорее/.	As soon as possible.
	Az soon az PAHS-ih-bl.
Как только ты захочешь.	As soon as you want.
	Az soon az yoo wahnt.
В будущем....	In the future...
	In th'FYOO-chur...

Two heads are better than one.

Один ум хорошо, а два лучше

Количество

Qu<u>a</u>ntities

Сколько лет/ сестре/ маме/ папе/?

How old is/ sister/ mommy/ daddy/?
Haou ohld iz/ SIS-ter/ MAHM-ee/ DAD-ee/?

Сколько пальцев ты видишь?

How many fingers do you see?
Haou MEN-ee FEENG-erz doo yoo see?

Сколько?

How many are there?
Haou MEN-ee ahr thehr?

Есть (только)/ один/ четыре/.

There is (only)/ one/ four/.
Thehr iz (OHN-lee) /wuhn/ for/.

У меня нет ничего.
Ничего нет!

I have none. There is nothing!
Igh hav nuhn. Thehr iz NUHTH- 'ng!

Всё печенье съели!

All the cookies have been eaten!
Awl th'KUK-eez hav ben EET-en!

Количество

После семи идёт восемь.

After seven comes eight.
AF-ter SEV-en kuhmz eit.

Считай от трёх до десяти.

Count from 3 to 10.
Kaount fruhm three too ten.

Продолжай считать.

Continue counting.
Kuhn-TIN-yoo KAOUNT- 'ng.

Один плюс один – два.

One and one makes two.
Wuhn and wuhn meiks too.

Сколько будет пять минус два?

How much is five minus two?
Haou muhch iz fighv MIGH-nis too?

Четыре минус один – три.

Four minus one is three.
For MIGH-nis wuhn iz three.

Дважды два – четыре.

Two times two equals four.
Too tighmz too EE-kwuhlz for.

Сорок разделить на пять – восемь.

Forty divided by five makes eight.
FORT-ee d'VIGHD-ed bigh fighv meiks eit.

Два, четыре, и шесть – чёртные числа.

Two, four and six are even numbers.
Too, for, and siks ahr EE-ven NUHM-berz.

Три, пять, и семь – нечёртные числа.

Three, five and seven are uneven numbers.
Three, fighv and SEV-en ahr UHN-eev-en NUHM-berz.

Две половины.

Two halves.
Too havz.

Дроби: половина, треть, четверть, три четверти.

Fractions: a half, a third, a fourth, three-fourths.
FRAK-shuhnz: uh haf, uh therd, uh forth, three-forths.

немного/ меньше/ больше/

a little/ less/ more/
uh LIT-ul/ les/ mor/

несколько

some, a few, several
suhm, uh fyoo, SEV-rul

много

many, a lot
MEN-ee, uh laht

zero	0	fourteen	14
ZIR-oh		*FOR-teen*	
one	1	fifteen	15
wuhn		*FIF-teen*	
two	2	sixteen	16
too		*SIKS-teen*	
three	3	seventeen	17
three		*SEV-en-teen*	
four	4	eighteen	18
for		*EIT-teen*	
five	5	nineteen	19
fighv		*NIGHN-teen*	
six	6	twenty	20
siks		*TWENT-ee*	
seven	7	twenty-one	21
SEV-en		*TWENT-ee-wuhn*	
eight	8	twenty-two	22
eit		*TWENT-ee-too*	
nine	9	twenty-three	23
nighn		*TWENT-ee-three*	
ten	10	thirty	30
ten		*THIRT-ee*	
eleven	11	thirty-one	31
ee-LEV-en		*THIRT-ee-wuhn*	
twelve	12	thirty-two	32
twelv		*THIRT-ee-too*	
thirteen	13	thirty-three	33
THIR-teen		*THIRT-ee-three*	

forty	40		ninety	90
FORT-ee			*NIGHNT-ee*	
forty-one	41		ninety-one	91
FORT-ee-wuhn			*NIGHNT-ee-wuhn*	
forty-two	42		ninety-two	92
FORT-ee-too			*NIGHNT-ee-too*	
forty-three	43		ninety-three	93
FORT-ee-three			*NIGHNT-ee-three*	
fifty	50		one hundred	100
FIF-tee			*wuhn HUHN-dred*	
fifty-one	51		one hundred one	101
FIF-tee-wuhn			*wuhn HUHN-dred wuhn*	
firty-two	52		one hundred two	102
FIF-tee-too			*wuhn HUHN-dred too*	
fifty-three	53		one hundred three	103
FIF-tee-three			*wuhn HUHN-dred three*	
sixty	60		two hundred	200
SIK-stee			*too HUHN-dred*	
sixty-one	61		two hundred one	201
SIK-stee-wuhn			*too HUHN-dred wuhn*	
sixty-two	62		two hundred two	202
SIK-stee-too			*too HUHN-dred too*	
sixty-three	63		two hundred	203
SIK-stee-three			*too HUHN-dred three*	
seventy	70		three hundred	300
SEV-en-tee			*three HUHN-dred*	
seventy-one	71		three hundred one	301
SEV-en-tee-wuhn			*three HUHN-dred wuhn*	
seventy-two	72		three hundred two	302
SEV-en-tee-too			*three HUHN-dred too*	
seventy-three	73		three hundred three	303
SEV-en-tee-three			*three HUHN-dred three*	
eighty	80		four hundred	400
EIT-ee			*for HUHN-dred*	
eighty-one	81		four hundred one	401
EIT-ee-wuhn			*for HUHN-dred wuhn*	
eighty-two	82		four hundred two	402
EIT-ee-too			*for HUHN-dred too*	
eighty-three	83		four hundred three	403
EIT-ee-three			*for HUHN-dred three*	

five hundred	500
fighv HUHN-dred	
five hundred one	501
fighv HUHN-dred wuhn	
five hundred two	502
fighv HUHN-dred too	
five hundred three	503
fighv HUHN-dred three	
six hundred	600
siks HUHN-dred	
six hundred one	601
siks HUHN-dred wuhn	
six hundred two	602
siks HUHN-dred too	
six hundred three	603
siks HUHN-dred three	
seven hundred	700
SEV-en HUHN-dred	
seven hundred one	701
SEV-en HUHN-dred wuhn	
seven hundred two	702
SEV-en HUHN-dred too	
seven hundred three	703
SEV-en HUHN-dred three	
eight hundred	800
eit HUHN-dred	
eight hundred one	801
eit HUHN-dred wuhn	
eight hundred two	802
eit HUHN-dred too	
eight hundred three	803
eit HUHN-dred three	

nine hundred	900
nighn HUHN-dred	
nine hundred one	901
nighn HUHN-dred wuhn	
nine hundred two	902
nighn HUHN-dred too	
nine hundred three	903
nighn HUHN-dred three	
one thousand	1000
wuhn THAOU-zand	
two thousand	2000
too THAOU-zand	
three thousand five hundred	3500
three THAOU-zand fighv HUHN-dred	
(or)	
thirty-five hundred	3500
THIRT-ee-fighv HUHN-dred	
ten thousand	10,000
ten THAOU-zand	
one hundred thousand	100,000
wuhn HUHN-dred THAOU-zand	
one million	1,000,000
wuhn MIL-yuhn	
two million	2,000,000
too MIL-yuhn	
one billion	1,000,000,000
wuhn BIL-yuhn	

Repetition is the mother of learning.

Повторенье — Мать ученья

Алфавит   ## Alphabet

A a	B b	C c	D d	E e	F f	G g
ei	bee	see	dee	ee	ef	jee
H h	I i	J j	K k	L l	M m	N n
eich	igh	jei	kei	el	em	en
O o	P p	Q q	R r	S s	T t	U u
oh	pee	kyoo	ahr	es	tee	yoo
V v	W w	X x	Y y	Z z		
vee	double yoo	eks	wigh	zee		

Какая это буква ?

What letter is this?
Waht LET-er iz this?

Вот буква А.

Here is the letter A.
Heer iz th'LET-er ei.

Назови эту букву.

Name this letter.
Neim this LET-er.

Сколько букв в слове "кошка"?

How many letters are in the word "cat"?
Haou MEN-ee LET-erz ahr in th'werd "kat"?

Где буква "Н"?

Where is the letter "N"?
Wehr iz th'LET-er "N"?

Скажи слово "легко" по буквам.

Spell the word "easy."
Spel th'werd "EE-zee."

Покажи букву "Г."

Point to the letter "G."
Poynt t'th'LET-er "jee."

Что значит это слово?

What does this word mean?
Waht duhz this werd meen?

Тебе нужно вычеркнуть это слово.

You have to cross out this word.
Yoo hav t'kraws aout this werd.

Чьё это имя?

Whose name is this?
Hooz neim iz this?

Не держи так крепко карандаш.

Don't hold the pencil tightly.
Dohnt hohld th'PEN-sil TIGHT-lee.

Держи его вот так.

Hold it like this.
Hohld it lighk this.

Пиши вот так.

Write like this.
Right lighk this.

Ты умеешь писать?

Do you know how to write?
Doo yoo noh haou t'right?

Я умею писать.

I know how to write.
Igh noh haou t'right.

what you sow you shall reap.

Что посеешь, то и пожнёшь

Детские песенки   Nursery Rhymes

Nursery rhymes are a marvelous way to soothe a crying baby, or just enjoy
for their own rhythm. (The English rhymes are not necessarily a translation
of the Russian rhymes.)

У Маши был барашек   Mary Had a Little Lamb

У Маши был барашек,   Mary had a little lamb
Барашек, барашек,   Its fleece was white as snow;

У Маши был барашек   And everywhere that Mary went,
С шёрсткой, словно снег.   The lamb was sure to go.

Куда бы Маша ни пошла,   It followed her to school one day,
Ни пошла, ни пошла,   That was against the rule;

Куда бы Маша ни пошла   It made the children laugh and play
Барашек ходит с ней.   To see the lamb at school.

Дождик, дождик, уходи

Дождик, дождик, уходи
Послезавтра приходи.
Разве трудно перестать?
Ваня хочет поиграть.

Rain, Rain Go Away

Rain, rain, go away.
Come again another day.
Little Johnny wants to play.

Пётр и Егорка

Пётр и Егорка
Полезли на горку,
Тащили ведёрко с водою.
Егорка свалился
И лбом приложился.
Петра потащил за собою.

Jack and Jill

Jack and Jill
Went up the hill
To fetch a pail of water;
Jack fell down
And broke his crown,
And Jill came tumbling after.

Прошу я звёздочку

Прошу я звёздочку мерцать,
Я так хочу её понять.
Над высоким миром, там,
Как алмаз сияет нам.
Прошу я звёздочку мерцать,
Я так хочу её понять.

Twinkle, Twinkle Little Star

Twinkle, twinkle, little star
How I wonder what you are!
Up above the world so high,
Like a diamond in the sky.

Просыпайся

Просыпайся, просыпайся,
Брат Антон, брат Антон.
Утро в колокольчик,
Утро в колокольчик
– Динь, динь, дон.
– Динь, динь, дон.

Brother John

Are you sleeping?
Are you sleeping?
Brother John, Brother John?
Morning bells are ringing.
Morning bells are ringing.
Ding, Ding, Dong.
Ding, Ding, Dong.

Детские песенки_____

Шалтай - Болтай

Шалтай - Болтай сидел на стене,
Шалтай - Болтай свалился во сне.
Ни царские кони,
ни царская рать
Не могут Шалтая - Болтая собрать.

Humpty Dumpty

Humpty Dumpty sat on a wall,
Humpty Dumpty had a great fall;
All the king's horses,
And all the king's men,
Couldn't put Humpty together
again.

Школьник, школьник,

Школьник, школьник,
Что так рано
Ты спешишь
Сегодня в класс?
Ты всегда
Приходишь в восемь,
А теперь
Десятый час!

Ten o'Clock Scholar

A dillar, a dollar,
A ten o'clock scholar,
What makes you come so soon?
You used to come at ten o'clock,
But now you come at noon.

Джек был героем

Джек был героем —
Он через свечку
Прыгнул однажды,
Забравшись на печку.

Jack Be Nimble

Jack, be nimble,
Jack, be quick,
Jack, jump over
      The candlestick.

В город

В город , в город за свиньёй
Я иду пешком.
Возвращаюсь я домой
На свинье верхом!

To Market, To Market

To market, to market
To buy a fat pig,
Home again, home again,
      jiggety-jig;
To market, to market
To buy a fat hog,
Home again, home again
      jiggety-jog.

160

Шалунишки– котятки

Шалунишки– котятки
    потеряли перчатки
И не смеют взойти на порог.
— Мама, мама, прости!
Мы не можем найти,
Куда подевались перчатки!
— Не найдёте перчатки,
так и знайте, котятки,
Я не стану готовить пирог!
Мяу-мяу пирог, мяу-мяу пирог,
Я не стану готовить пирог!

Испугались котятки,
отыскали перчатки
И к маме бегут со всех ног.

— Мама, мама, открой
и пусти нас домой!
Мы нашли на дороге перчатки!
— Отыскали перчатки?
Золотые котятки!
Получайте за это пирог!
Мяу-мяу пирог, мяу-мяу пирог,
Получайте за это пирог!

Натянули котятки
на лапки перчатки
И съели до крошки пирог.
— Ай, мамочка, ай!
Ты нас не ругай,
Но грязными стали перчатки!
— Грязнульки-котятки!
Снимайте перчатки!
Я вас посажу под замок!
Мяу-мяу под замок,
мяу-мяу под замок,
Я вас посажу под замок!

Three Little Kittens

Three little kittens
They lost their mittens,
    And they began to cry.
Oh, Mother dear,
We sadly fear
Our mittens we have lost.
What! Lost your mittens,
You naughty kittens!
Then you shall have no pie.
    Meow, Meow, Meow.
No, you shall have no pie.

The three little kittens,
They found their mittens,
    And they began to cry,
Oh, Mother dear,
See here, see here,
Our mittens we have found.
Put on your mittens,
You silly kittens,
And you shall have some pie.
Meow, Meow, Meow,
Oh, let us have some pie.

The three little kittens
Put on their mittens
And soon ate up the pie;
Oh, Mother dear,
We greatly fear
Our mittens we have soiled.
What! Soiled your mittens,
You naughty kittens!
Then they began to sigh,
Meow, Meow, Meow,
Then they began to sigh.

161

Детские песенки

Стирают котятки
в корыте перчатки.
Ах, как это трудно – стирать!
Все три, три и три –
Ой, мама, смотри!
Уже отстирались перчатки!
— Отмыли перчатки?
За это, котятки,
Я вас отпущу погулять!
Мяу-мяу погулять,
Мяу-мяу погулять,
Опять отпущу погулять!

The three little kittens
They washed their mittens,
    And hung them out to dry;
Oh, Mother dear,
Do you not hear,
Our mittens we have washed.
What! Washed your mittens,
You good little kittens,
But I smell a rat close by.
Meow, Meow, Meow,
We smell a rat close by.

Три беленькие мышки

Три беленькие мышки
Бегут, не чуя ног,
За мельничихой старой
Вприпрыжку за порог.

Она хвосты отрезала
Им кухонным ножом
А что случилось дальше,
Я расскажу потом.

Three Blind Mice

Three blind mice,
See how they run!
They all ran after the farmer's wife,
Who cut off their tails
With a carving knife,
Did you ever see,
Such a sight in your life,
As three blind mice?

Баю - баю, детки

Баю - баю, детки
На еловой ветке.
Тронет ветер вашу ель —
Закачает колыбель,
А подует во весь дух —
Колыбель на землю — бух!

Rock-a-Bye Baby

Rock-a-bye, baby
On a tree top,
When the wind blows,
The cradle will rock;
When the bough breaks,
The cradle will fall;
Down will come baby,
Cradle and all.

МОЛИТВЫ

Отче Наш

Отче наш, сущий на небесах,
Да святится имя Твое;
Да придет Царствие Твое;
Да будет воля твоя и на земле,
как на небе;
Хлеб наш насущный
дай нам на сей день;
и прости нам долги наши,
как и мы прощаем
должникам нашим;
и не введи нас в искушение,
но избавь нас от лукавого. Аминь.

Псалом Давида

1. Господь– Пастырь мой
я ни в чем не буду нуждаться:
2. Он покоит меня на злачных
пажитях и водит меня
к водам тихим,
3. Подкрепляет душу мою,
направляет меня на стези правды
ради имени Своего.
4. Если я пойду и долиною
смертной тени, не убоюсь зла,
потому что Ты со мною;
Твой жезл и Твой посох– они
успокоивают меня.
5. Ты приготовил
предо мною трапезу
в виду врагов моих,
умастил елеем голову мою;
чаша моя преисполнена.
6. Так, благость и милость да
сопровождают меня во все дни
жизни мой, и я пребуду в доме
Господнем многие дни.

Молитва перед едой

Благослови, Господи, все, что
по милости твоей вкушаем.
Аминь.

PRAYERS

Our Father

Our Father, who are in heaven,
hallowed be thy name; Thy
kingdom come, Thy will be
done on earth
as it is in heaven.
Give us this day;
Our daily bread,
and forgive us our trespasses
as we forgive those
who trespass against us
And lead us not into temptation,
but deliver us from evil. Amen.

Psalm 23

1. The Lord is my shepherd;
    there is nothing I lack.
2. In green pastures you let me lie;
    to safe waters you lead me;
    you restore my strength.
3. You guide me along the right path
    for the sake of your name.
4. Even when I walk in a dark valley,
    I fear no evil for you are with me;
    your rod and your staff give me
    courage.
5. You set a table before me
    in the sight of my foes;
    You anoint my head with oil;
    my cup overflows.
6. Only goodness and kindness
    will pursue me
    all the days of my life;
    I will dwell in the house of the Lord
    for years to come.

Prayer before Meals

Thank you Lord for all the
kindness and nourishment
you provide. Amen.

Словарь/VOCABULARY

Словарь

Семья и другие лица

мать/ мама	mother/ mom
отец/ папа	father/ dad
бабушка	grandmother
дедушка	grandfather
неродной брат	cousin (m)
неродная сестра	cousin (f)
жена	wife
муж	husband
тётя	aunt
дядя	uncle
племянница	niece
племянник	nephew
внучка	grand-daughter

The Family and Other Persons

внук	grandson
дочь	daughter
сын	son
сестра	sister
брат	brother
женщина	woman
мужчина	man
девочка	girl
мальчик	boy
ребёнок	child
господин	Mister
госпожа	Missus
госпожа	Miss

Ласковые слова

мой/ моя детка	my baby
моя кукла	my doll
моя принцесса	my princess
мой принц	my prince
моё сокровище	my treasure
дорогой (мой)	sweetheart

Endearments

дорогая (моя)	sweetheart
дружок	buddy
моя малышка	my little one
мой малыш	my little one
милый (ая)	honey, sweetie
мой цыплёнок	my little chick

Цвета

зелёный	green
синий	blue
чёрный	black
белый	white
оранжевый	orange
красный	red

Colors

жёлтый	yellow
Фиолетовый	purple
розовый	pink
коричневый	brown
серый	gray
бежевый	beige

Дни недели

понедельник	Monday
вторник	Tuesday
среда	Wednesday
четверг	Thursday

Days of the Week

пятница	Friday
суббота	Saturday
воскресенье	Sunday

Словарь

Месяца

январь	January
февраль	February
март	March
апрель	April
май	May
июнь	June

Months of the Year

июль	July
август	August
сентябрь	September
октябрь	October
ноябрь	November
декабрь	December

Времена года

весна	spring
лето	summer (m)

Seasons of the Year

осень	autumn
зима	winter

Праздники года

день рождения	birthday
Новый год	New Year's
день Св. Валентина	Valentine's Day
Еврейская пасха	Passover
пасха	Easter

Holidays of the Year

день Матери	Mother's Day
день Отца	Father's Day
4-е июля	July 4
празник всех святых	Halloween
день благодарения	Thanksgiving Day
рождество	Christmas
сочельник	Christmas Eve

Детская комната

ванна	bath tub
книга	book
коляска	carriage
детская кроватка	crib
пелёнка	diaper
бутылочка	bottle
стульчик для кормления	high chair
Мать Гусыня	Mother Goose

Nursery

ночник	night light
пустышка	pacifier
картина	picture
манеж	play pen
горшок	potty
качалка	rocker
английская булавка	safety pin
коляска	stroller
игрушка	toy

Игрушки

Toys

мяч	ball
воздушный шар	balloon
бита	bat
бусина	bead
велосипед	bicycle
кубик	block
(парусная) лодка	boat (sail)
бульдозер	bull dozer
автобус	bus
автомобиль	car
шахматная доска	chess board
глина	clay
клоун	clown
ковбой	cowboy
цветной карандаш	crayon
кукла	doll
кукольный дом	doll house
барабан	drum
серьга	earring
удочка	fishing rod
форт	fort
игра	game
глобус	globe
вертолёт	helicopter
обруч	hoop
труба	horn
индеец	Indian
чёртик в табакерке	jack-in-the box
скакалка	jump rope
воздушный змей	kite
стеклянный шарик	marble
маска	mask
ожерелье	necklace
набор красок	paint box

кисточка	paint brush
клейстер	paste
книга с картинками	picture book
копилка	piggy bank
самолёт	plane
марионетка	puppet
пузл	puzzle
гоночный автомобиль	race car
грабли	rake
погремушка	rattle
кольцо	ring
ракета	rocket
конь-качалка	rocking horse
верёвка	rope
песочница	sandbox
ножницы	scissors
самокат	scooter
качели	seesaw
лопатка	shovel
конёк	skate (ice)
роликовый конёк	skate(roller)
роликовая доска	skateboard
санки	sled
детская горка	slide
солдатик	soldier
подводная лодка	submarine
качели	swing
танк	tank (military)
чайный сервис	tea service
мишка	teddy
теннисная ракетка	tennis racquet
палатка	tent

Словарь

юла, волчок	top	нефтевоз	oil truck
ящик для игрушек	toy box	аварийная машина	tow truck
трактор	tractor	вагон	wagon
поезд	train	тачка	wheelbarrow
трёхколёсный велосипед	tricycle	свисток	whistle
грузовик	truck	ксилофон	xylophone
самосвал	dump truck		
пожарная машина	fire truck		
мусороуборочная машина	garbage truck		

Одежда

Clothes

рюкзак	backpack	резиновый сапог	rubber (boot)
купальный халат	bathrobe	сандалия	sandal
купальный костюм	bathing suit	шарф	scarf
плавки	bathing trunks	рубашка	shirt
ремень	belt	туфля	shoe
нагрудник	bib	шнурок	shoelace
блузка	blouse	шорты	shorts
сапог	boot	юбка	skirt
кепка	cap	комбинация	slip
пальто	coat	тапочка	slipper
платье	dress	кроссовки	sneakers
перчатка	glove	лыжный костюм	snow suit
носовой платок	handkerchief	носок	sock
шапка	hat	чулок	stocking
куртка	jacket	спортивный костюм	sweat suit
джинсы	jeans		
варежка	mitten	пуловер	sweater
ночная рубашка	nightgown	майка	tee-shirt
пальто	overcoat	галстук	tie
пижама	pajamas	колготки	tights
трусики	panties	зонт	umbrella
колготки	pantyhose	подштанники	underpants
штаны, брюки	pants	майка	undershirt
сумочка, кошелёк	pocketbook	нижнее бельё	underwear
плащ	rain coat	бумажник	wallet
		штормовка	windbreaker

168

Развлечения

луна-парк	amusement park
аквариум	aquarium
пляж	beach
бадминтон	badminton
бейсбол	baseball
баскетбол	basketball
кегельбан	bowling
поход	camping
цирк	circus
концерт	concert
езда на велосипеде	cycling
луна-парк	fairground
рыбалка	fishing
американский футбол	football
матч	game, match
гольф	golf
гимнастика	gymnastics
ходить в поход	hiking
фильм	movie
кино	movie theatre
музей	museum
парк	park

Entertainments

вечеринка	party
пикник	picnic
площадка	playground
чтение	reading
переменка	recess (school)
ресторан	restaurant
гребля	rowing
парусный спорт	sailing
ходить по магазинам	shopping
кататься на коньках	skating
футбол	soccer
спорт	sports
филателия	stamp collecting
плавание	swimming
теннис	tennis
театр	theatre
волейбол	volleyball
ходьба	walking
виндсерфинг	windsurfing
зоопарк	zoo

Тело человека

лодыжка	ankle
рука	arm
спина	back
живот	belly
пупок	belly button
щека	cheek
грудь	chest
подбородок	chin
ухо	ear
локоть	elbow
глаз	eye
бровь	eyebrow
веко	eyelid

Human Body

лицо	face
палец	finger
ноготь	finger nail
лоб	forehead
волосы	hair
рука	hand
голова	head
пятка	heel
бедро	hip
челюсть	jaw
колено	knee
нога	leg
губа	lip

Словарь

Тело человека

рот	mouth
шея	neck
нос	nose
плечо	shoulder
живот	stomach
горло	throat

Напитки

пиво	beer
какао	cocoa
кофе (с молоком)	coffee (with milk)
лимонад	lemonade
молоко	milk
апельсиновый сок	orange juice

Ёмкости

пакет	bag
бутылка	bottle
ящик	box
консервная банка	can
картонная коробка	carton
деревянный ящик	crate

Десерт

яблочный пирог	apple pie
торт	cake
леденец	candy
конфета	candy bar
шоколад	chocolate
печенье	cookie
круассон	croissant
заварной крем	custard
пончик, донатс	donut
желатин	gelatin
мороженое	ice cream

Human Body (cont.)

большой палец	thumb
палец на ноге	toe
язык	tongue
зуб	tooth
талия	waist
запястье	wrist

Beverages

апельсиновый напиток	orangeade
газированная вода	soda
чай с лимоном	tea with lemon
вода	water
вино	wine

Containers

конверт	envelope
банка	jar
крышка	top, cover
тюбик	tube
обёртка	wrapper

Dessert

фруктовый коктейль	milk shake
блин	pancake
пирожное	pastry
пирог	pie
пудинг	pudding
рисовый пудинг	rice pudding
бисквит	sponge cake
пирожок	turnover
йогурт	yoghurt

Овощи

Vegetables

спаржа	asparagus	лук	onion
свёкла	beet	петрушка	parsley
брюссельская	Brussel sprout	горох	pea
капуста		перец	pepper
капуста	cabbage	картофель	potato
морковь	carrot	тыква	pumpkin
цветная капуста	cauliflower	редис	radish
сельдерей	celery	шпинат	spinach
кукуруза	corn	кабачок	squash
огурец	cucumber	стручковая	stringbean
чеснок	garlic	фасоль	
салат	lettuce	помидор	tomato
гриб	mushroom	репа	turnip

Мясные блюда

Meat

бекон	bacon	баранья отбивная	lamb chop
курица	chicken	свиная отбивная	pork chop
сосиска	frankfurter	жаркое	roast
ветчина	ham	ростбиф	roast beef
гамбургер	hamburger	колбаса	sausage
сосиска в булке	hot dog	бифштекс	steak
нога баранья	leg of lamb	индейка	turkey

Рыбные блюда

Seafood

карп	carp	сардина	sardine
треска	cod	креветка	shrimp
камбала	flounder	палтус	sole
селёдка	herring	форель	trout
омар	lobster	тунец	tuna
лососина	salmon		

Словарь

Фрукты и ягоды

яблоко	apple
яблочное пюре	applesauce
абрикос	apricot
банан	banana
ягода	berry
черника	blueberry
черешня	cherry
кокосовый орех	coconut
виноградина	grape
грейпфрут	grapefruit
виноград кисть	grapes (bunch)

Fruits and Berries

лимон	lemon
апельсин	orange
персик	peach
груша	pear
ананас	pineapple
слива	plum
чернослив	prune
изюмина, изюм	raisin/s
малина	raspberry
клубника	strawberry
мандарин	tangerine
арбуз	watermelon

Другие продукты

хлеб	bread
сдобная булка	bun
масло	butter
каша	cereal (hot)
сыр	cheese
кукурузные хлопья	cornflakes
крекер	cracker
сливки	cream
крошка	crumb
яйцо	egg
глазунья	fried eggs
яйцо вкрутую	hard boiled egg
яйцо всмятку	soft boiled egg
картофель фри	French fries
подливка	gravy
мёд	honey
джем	jam, jelly
варенье	jam
кетчуп	ketchup
картофельное пюре	mashed potatoes
майонез	mayonaise
молочный шоколад	milk chocolate
горчица	mustard

Other Foods

макароны	noodles
овсяные хлопья	oatmeal
блин	pancake
арахис	peanut
арахисовая паста	peanut butter
перец	pepper
соленье	pickle
попкорн	pop-corn
картофельные чипсы	potato chips
рис	rice
булочка	roll
салат	salad
соль	salt
сандвич	sandwich
(с сыром)	(with cheese)
соус	sauce
квашеная капуста	sauerkraut
суп	soup
спагетти	spaghetti
тушёное мясо	stew
сироп	syrup
тост	toast
уксус	vinegar

Кухонные принадлежности

бутылка	bottle	кастрюля	pot
миска	bowl	кастрюля	saucepan
чашка	cup	блюдце	saucer
вилка	fork	неглубокая	skillet
стакан	glass	сковорода	
чайник	kettle	глубокая тарелка	soup plate
нож	knife	ложка	spoon
кружка	mug	скатерть	tablecloth
салфетка	napkin	столовая ложка	tablespoon
кувшин	pitcher	чайник	teapot
тарелка	plate	чайная ложка	teaspoon
блюдо	platter	поднос	tray

Utensils

Дом

чердак	attic	прихожая	hallway
задняя дверь	back door	шланг	hose
подвал	basement	кухня	kitchen
ванная	bathroom	газон	lawn
спальня	bedroom	разбрызгиватель	lawn sprinkler
потолок	ceiling	гостиная	living room
труба	chimney	почтовый ящик	mail box
столовая	dining room	крыша	roof
дверь	door	комната	room
семейная комната	family room	лестница	stair
забор	fence	ступенька	step
флаг	flag	унитаз	toilet
пол	floor	подсобка	utility room
входная дверь	front door	стена	wall
сад	garden	окно	window
калитка	gate	двор	yard

House

Жилище

квартира	apartment	дача	country house
бунгало	bungalow	гостиница	hotel
коттедж в лесу	cabin	палатка	tent
кооперативная	condominium	прицеп	trailer,
квартира			mobile home

Dwellings

Словарь

Кухня / Kitchen

передник	apron	микроволновка	microwave oven
метла	broom	швабра	mop
шкафчик для уборки	broom closet	духовка	oven
		ведро	pail
шкаф	cabinet, cupboard	кастрюля	pot
часы	clock	скороварка	pressure cooker
стенной шкаф	closet	холодильник	refrigerator
стиральная машина	clothes washer	швейная машина	sewing machine
компьютер	computer	раковина	sink
стол для готовки	counter	губка	sponge
моющее средство	detergent	табуретка	stool
тряпка	dish cloth	плита	stove
посудомоечная машина	dish washer	сито	strainer
		стол	table
тряпка для пыли	dust cloth	тостер	toaster
совок для мусора	dustpan	пылесос	vacuum cleaner
веничек	egg beater		
воронка	funnel	воск	wax
утюг	iron		
гладильная доска	ironing board		

Ванная комната / Bathroom

аспирин	aspirin	духи	perfume
банное полотенце	bath towel	пудра	powder
ванна	bathtub	бритва	razor
щётка для волос	brush	электробритва	razor (electric)
одеколон	cologne	шампунь	shampoo
расческа	comb	раковина	sink
личное полотенце	face cloth	мыло	soap
крем для лица	face cream	бумажная салфетки	tissues
фен	hair dryer	унитаз	toilet
губная помада	lipstick		
лак для ногтей	nail polish	туалетная бумага	toilet paper
бумажное полотенце	paper towel	зубная щётка	toothbrush
		зубная паста	toothpaste

174

Спальня

кресло	armchair
кровать	bed
покрывало	bedspread
ночной столик	bedside table
одеяло	blanket
жалюзи	blinds
ковёр	carpet
стул	chair
часы	clock
вешалка	coat hanger
занавеска	curtain
туалетный столик	dresser

Bedroom

лампа	lamp
абажур	lampshade
матрас	mattress
зеркало	mirror
подушка	pillow
наволочка	pillow case
розетка	outlet (electric)
лосткутное одеяло	quilt
кресло-качалка	rocking chair
простыня	sheet
ставень	shutter

Гостиная

кондиционер	air-conditioner
кресло	armchair
книжная полка	book shelf
книжный шкаф	bookcase
ковёр	carpet
диван	couch

Living Room

проигрыватель для компакт-дисков	CD player
письменный стол	desk
камин	fireplace
пианино	piano
картина	picture
радио	radio

Инструменты

топор	ax
молоток	hammer
шланг	hose
лестница	ladder
газонокосилка	lawn mower
гвоздь	nail
гайка	nut
вилы	pitchfork
плоскогубцы	pliers
грабли	rake
наждачная бумага	sandpaper

Tools

пила	saw
ножницы	scissors
винт	screw
отвёртка	screwdriver
лопата	shovel
мастерок	trowel
тиски	vise
тачка	wheelbarrow
гаечный ключ	wrench

175

Словарь

Машина

акселератор	accelerator
тормоз	brakes
бампер	bumper
приборная панель	dashboard
дверь	door
мотор	engine
бардачок	glove compartment
фара	headlight
капот	hood
гудок	horn
зажигание	ignition
домкрат	jack

The Car

зеркало обзора	mirror
заднее стекло	rear window
сиденье	seat
стартёр	starter
руль	steering wheel
противосолнеч- ный козырёк	sun visor
шина	tire
багажник	trunk
колесо	wheel
ветровое стекло	windshield
дворник	windshield wiper

Магазины

булочная	bakery
банк	bank
парикмахерская	barber shop
салон красоты	beauty shop
мясной магазин	butcher shop
химчистка	cleaners
магазин одежды	clothing store
магазин диети- ческих продуктов	dairy store
магазин деликатесов	deli
универмаг	department store
аптека	drugstore

Stores

рыбный рынок	fish market
цветочный маг.	florist
мебельный маг.	furniture store
заправочная станция	gas station
гастроном	grocery store
скобяной маг.	hardware store
ювелирный маг.	jewelry store
прачечная	laundromat
склад лесоматериалов	lumber yard
питомник	nursery
обувной маг.	shoe store
маг. игрушек	toy store

Профессии

астронавт	astronaut
(приходящая) няня	baby sitter
пекарь	baker
парикмахер	barber
водитель(автобуса)	(bus) driver

Occupations

мясник	butcher
плотник	carpenter
шофёр	chauffeur
уборщица	cleaning lady

повар	cook	медбрат (m)	nurse
молочник	dairy man	медсестра (f)	nurse
молочница	dairy woman	маляр	painter
магазина	deli shop owner	фармацевт	pharmacist
деликатесов		пилот	pilot
зубной врач	dentist	полицейский	policeman
врач	doctor	женщина-	police-
инженер	engineer	полицейский	woman
фермер	farmer	священник	priest
пожарник	fireman	гонщик	race car driver
автомеханик	garage mechanic	моряк	sailor
мусорщик	garbage man	продавец	salesman
садовник	gardener	продавщица	saleswoman
бакалейщик	grocer	секретарь	secretary
парикмахер	hairdresser	таксист	taxi driver
домашняя	housewife	учитель	teacher
хозяйка		учительница	teacher
ювелир	jeweler	машинист	train engineer
адвокат	lawyer	билетёр	usher
библиотекарь	librarian	билетёрша	usherette
горничная	maid	официант	waiter
почтальон	mailman	официантка	waitress
торговец	merchant	работник	zoo keeper
священник	minister	зоопарка	
манекенщик	model		
манекенщинца	model		

Насекомые

Insects

муравей	ant	мошка	gnat
шмель	bumblebee	кузнечик	grasshopper
бабочка	butterfly	медоносная	honey bee
гусеница	caterpillar	пчела	
цикада	cicada	божья коровка	lady bug
таракан	cockroach	комар	mosquito
сверчок	cricket	мотылёк	moth
стрекоза	dragonfly	богомол	praying mantis
блоха	flea	паук	spider
муха	fly	оса	wasp

Словарь

Деревья

яблоня	apple
берёза	birch
черешня	cherry
фруктовое дерево	fruit tree
болиголов	hemlock
клён	maple
дуб	oak

Trees

грушевое дер.	pear
сосна	pine
сливовое дер.	plum
тополь	poplar
секвойя	sequoia
ель	spruce
ива	willow

Животные

медведь	bear
бык	bull
верблюд	camel
кошка	cat
курица	chick
корова	cow
крокодил	crocodile
олень	deer
собака	dog
осёл	donkey
утка	duck
слон	elephant
молодой олень	fawn
лиса	fox
пудель	French poodle
лягушка	frog
жираф	giraffe
козёл	goat
горилла	gorilla
гусь	goose
морская свинка	guinea pig
хомяк	hamster
гиппопотам	hippopotamus
лошадь	horse
ягнёнок	lamb
леопард	leopard
лев	lion

Animals

лама	llama
крот	mole
обезьяна	monkey
мышь	mouse
вол	ox
свинья	pig
поросёнок	piglet
пони	pony
щенок	puppy
заяц	rabbit
енот	raccoon
крыса	rat
северный олень	reindeer
петух	rooster
тюлень	seal
овца	sheep
змея	snake
белка	squirrel
тигр	tiger
индюк	turkey
черепаха	turtle
кит	whale
волк	wolf
червь	worm
(земляной)	(earth)
зебра	zebra

Птицы

дрозд	blackbird	сова	owl
синяя птица	bluebird	попугай	parrot
канарейка	canary	павлин	peacock
кардинал	cardinal	пеликан	pelican
цыплёнок	chick	пингвин	penguin
курица	chicken	фазан	pheasant
ворона	crow	голубь	pigeon
утка	duck	ворон	raven
утёнок	duckling	зарянка	robin
орёл	eagle	чайка	seagull
гусь	goose	воробей	sparrow
гусёнок	gosling	аист	stork
колибри	hummingbird	ласточка	swallow
жаворонок	lark	лебедь	swan
соловей	nightingale	индюк	turkey
страус	ostrich	дятел	woodpecker

Цветы

азалия	azalea	ландыш	lily of the valley
лютик	buttercup		
гвоздика	carnation	мимоза	mimosa
первоцвет	cowslip	хризантема	mum
шафран	crocus	орхидея	orchid
нарцисс	daffodil	анютины глазки	pansy
георгин	dahlia	пион	peony
маргаритка	daisy	петуния	petunia
одуванчик	dandelion	рододендрон	rhododendron
гардения	gardenia	роза	rose
герань	geranium	подсолнечник	sunflower
ирис	iris	душистый горошек	sweet pea
сирень	lilac	тюльпан	tulip
лилия	lily	фиалка	violet

Birds

Flowers

Словарь

Вдоль дороги

Along the Road

аэропорт	airport	моторолер	motorscooter
небольшая авария	breakdown	ставить на стоянку	to park
мост	bridge	пешеход	pedestrian
здание	building	почта	post office
многоквартирный дом	apartment building	дорога	road
здание под офисы	office building	дорожный знак	road sign
автобус (школьный)	bus (school)	тротуар	sidewalk
автобусная станция	bus station	снегоуборочный комбайн	snowplow
автобусная остановка	bus stop	снегоход	snow mobile
машина	car	ограничение скорости	speed limit
церковь	church	спортивная машина	sports car
угол	corner	улица	street
бордюр	curb	уличный фонарь	street light
скоростная автострада	expressway	такси	taxi
фабрика	factory	телефонная будка	telephone booth
забор	fence	телефонный столб	telephone pole
поле	field	пути (железнодорожные)	tracks (railroad)
пожарное депо	fire house	движение	traffic
пожарный насос	fire plug	кольцевая транспортная развязка	traffic circle
спущенная шина	flat tire	пробка	traffic jam
живая изгородь	hedge	светофор	traffic light
автострада	highway	поезд	train
ехать автостопом	hitch-hiking	вокзал	train station
дом	house	грузовик	truck
почтовый ящик	mail box	аварийная машина	tow truck
мопед	moped	туннель	tunnel
мотоцикл	motorbike, motorcycle	микроавтобус	van

Руководство по произошению Pronunciation Guide

Английское Произношение

Vowels: Гласные:

буква	знак	Английский Пример	Руссский Пример
a	ah	father	Mama
a	ei	ate	Эй-Би-Си
a	u	ago	амбар
			часть
e	e	get	этот
e	ee	easy	жить
e	ehr	where	мёрзнуть
i	i	big	кисть
i	igh	high	лайка
o	ah	not	хот-дог
o	aw	saw	очень
o	aou	how	аудит
o	oh	goh	гол
o	oy	boy	бойкий
u	u	put	бублик
u	oo	you	улица

Руководство по произошению Pronunciation Guide

Consonants: Согласные:

буква	знак	Английский Пример	Руссский Пример
b	b	ball	бабка
d	d	dad	дом
g	g	go	гол
h	h	he	хижина
j	j	judge	жить
k	k	king	комбайн
l	l	look	лайка
m	m	man	муж
n	n	not	нет
p	p	play	подарок
r	r	run	рано
s	s	see	сад
t	t	tea	такси
v	v	van	волос
w	w	what	-------
x	eks	excellent	индекс
z	zee	zebra	зебра

Note: The pronunciation given in <u>Kids Stuff Angliiski (English)</u> is English recognizable to any English-speaking person.

Индекс /INDEX

А

аккумулятор	battery 99
аккуратно	gently 102
апельсинный сок	orange juice 33
аптека	drugstore 83

Б

бабушка	grandma 38, 56
бак для мусора	garbage pail 68
банан	banana 31
барабан	to bang a drum 39
барбекю	barbecue 48
бассейн	pool 93, 114
Безусловно!	Sure! 125
бекон	bacon 29
беспокоиться	to worry 127
беспокойство	trouble 45
беспорядок	mess 128
библиотека	library 60,112
билет	ticket 108, 118
билетная касса	ticket office 118
Бис!	Encore! 80
бита	bat 94
благодарен	thankful 80
блуска	blouse 25
блюдо	dish 50
Бог	God 17,130
болеть голова	headache 140
болеть	to ache 140
болеть зуб	toothache 140
болеть	to hurt 39,43,54,141,142
больше нравиться	to prefer 88
большой	immense 130
большой	a lot 17
большой	large 36, 103
борный	rough 115
босой	barefoot 58
ботинок	shoe 25
бояться	(to be) afraid 40,61,127
брат	brother 36,50,57,116
брать	to rent 117
бросить (вы)	to throw 50,68,77,94,96
бросок	throw 94
брызгать	to splash 22
брюки	pants 25
бубенчик	bell 39

Б

букв	letter (alpha) 156,157
бумага	paper 77,100,101
бык	bull 103
быстро	fast 31,39,95,98

В

в будущем	(In the) future 150
В порядке!	O.K! 121
вагон	wagon 69, 93
ваниль	vanilla 135
ванна	bath 21,23
ведро	pail 115
Везёт!	Lucky! 126
великодушен	generous 79
велосипед	bicycle 94,95,96
верёка	tail 104
вернуть	to return(an item)60,84
вернуться	to come back 44, 75
весело	to have a good time 120
весело	fun 111
весело	happy 122
весло	oar 98
вести	to behave 53
ветер	wind 104, 145
ветрено	windy 145
вечеринка	party 132,133,135
взбивать	to beat 66
взбираться	to climb trees 93
Вздор!	Nonsense! 126
взять	to take 30, 35
взять	to use 100
видеть	to see 14,21,36,37, 50,107,108,147
вилка	fork 31
виноватый	(to be at) fault 122
включить	to sound 105
включить	to turn on light 576
вкусный	delicious 33
вместе	together 58, 107
вниз	downstairs 55,56
вовнутрь	inside 119
вовремя	(on) time 61
вода	water 21,22,32,99, 115,116,163

В

водительские права	driver's license 109,135
воздушный шар	balloon 105, 133
воздушный змей	kite 104
войти	to come in 14, 56
вокруг	around 105
волосы	hair 113
вопрос	question 73, 74
вот	Here is 40,67,103, 115,156
Вофсайде!	Off sides! 106
вперёд	forward 97
впредь будь	from now on 48
врач	doctor 40, 91
время	time 44,72,76
все	everyone 135
всё	to be all right 15
всё	everything 33,55,120,128
вставать	to get up 24, 42
встать	to stand up 51,105
встретиться	to meet 88,114
вход	entrance 89
вчера	yesterday 71
выглядеть	to look, appear 23,26,79
выиграть	to win 97
выиграть	to score 94
выйти	to come out 115
выйти	to get out 98
выключить	to turn out 22,59
вылетать	to take off (airplane) 92
выносить	to take out 61
вынуть	to pull out 41
вырасти счёт	to run up (bill) 60
выставка	exhibit 112
высунуть	to stick out 141
вытереть	to dry 22
вытирать (пыль)	to dust 65
вытирать	to wipe 54,58
выучить	to know a lesson 77
выход	exit 89
вычистить	to clean 22
вычеркнуть	to cross out 157
вышка	diving board 93

Г

гараж	garage 100
глина	clay 101

Г

гастроном	grocery store 83
гвоздь	nail 69,114
где	where 103,117,133(+)
гладить	to iron 66
глаз	eye 36,40,52,79,104
гластырь	bandaid 142
глоточек	sip 32
глупо	silly 122
говорить	to speak 14,18,32,35, 45,50,53,71,124
гол	goal 89,106
голова	head 35,54,141
голоден	hungry 28
голос	voice 78
гоняться	to chase 103
гордиться	(to be) proud 81
горка	hill 118, 159
горький	bitter 32
гостиная	living room 56
готов	ready 29,39,105,(+)
готово	done 66
град	hail 146
грести	to row 98
греть/ся (со)	to warm up 29,119
грипп	flu 141
гроза	storm 146
гром	thunder 146
грузовик	truck 108,109
грязный	dirty 19,42,50,64
грязь	dirt 93
гулять (по)	to take walk 39,41,119
гусеница	caterpilllar 68

Д

давай(те)	Let's go 39,71,99,119
давать	to let 26,31,37,87,95
давать по очерели	to take turns 45,115
дать	to give 42,57
дверь	door 46
двигать	to move 36,44,63
движение	traffic 95,119
двор	yard 90,93,94,114
девочка	girl 79, 126
дезодорант	deodorant 22

Д

делать	to do 28,45,51,57,59
делиться (по)	to share 30,115
день	day 14,18,71,117
день рождения	birthday 132-135
деньги	money 86
дерево	tree 68,93,107
дерево	wood 69
держать/ся	to hold 35,37,41,48, 94,95,104,105,157
держаться за	to take 41
держаться	to stay away 48
дешевле	cheaper 86
джип	pick-up(truck) 109
длинный	long 37
длиться	to last 150
добрый	generous 79
добрый	nice 18
довольно	enough 76, 128
дождать (по)	to wait for 44,49
дождь	rain 145,147
должен	should 45,50,60,73,136
должен	to have to 97
доллар	dollar 85
дом	house 43,64
дом на дереве	tree house 114
дом	home 61,71,111,119,133
домашняя работа	homework 60
дорога	way 56
дорогой	expensive 86
доска	board 69, 114
доставлять	to deliver 1098
достаточно	enough 93,104
дразнить	to tease 46
драться	to fight 45
друг/-а	friend 60,91,133
думать	to think 35,36,49,54, 55,89,107
духовка	oven 66
дырокол	hole punch 74
дышать	breathe 54
дядя	uncle 75

Е

закрыть	to put down 20
еда	food 31
ездить на велосипеде	to ride (bike) 95

Е

есть	there is 30,31,112,151
есть (съ)	to eat 27,29,31,33,39, 67,112,115,119,151
ехать	to go (move) 99
ещё	yet, still 137,139
ещё	another 30
ещё раз	again 80

Ж

жалоба	complaint 62
жаловаться	to complain 130
жаль	pity, sorrow 122,126
жар	fever 141
жарко	hot 145
Желаю успеха!	Good luck! 17
железа	gland 141
жёлтый	yellow 100
животик	tummy 21,37
животное	animal 72,103,178
журнал	magazine 100

З

за	after 71,106
за	behind 89, 94, 108
забить	to score 106
забыть	to forget 20, 55
завернуть	to wrap 67
завтра	tomorrow 14,71,142
завтракать	to breakfast 27
задать вопрос	to ask a question 73,74
задний	back 100
задний ход	backwards 108
задуть	to blow out 134
зажигать	to light 48,56
закончить	to finish 111,114
закрыть	to turn off faucet 21
закрыть	to close 46,58,104,138
залезть	to climb 41
замелчатель-ный	great 80
замечателен	wonderful 80
Замечательно!	Marvelous! 127
замок за песка	sand castle 116
замок	castle 116
заниматься	to study 73

З

занятой	busy 43
заняться	to busy 76
запачкать	to stain 57
запереть	to lock 46
заплатить	to pay 97
заправочная станция	gas station 83
Заправьте!	Fill 'er up! 100
заслуживать	to deserve 77
застегнуть	to button 25
застегнуть	to zipper 25
застрять	stuck 74
затупиться	dull 105
заходить	to go in 43, 119
звонить	to name 18,102
звонить (по)	to call 14,105,113
здесь	here 68,88,103,115,117
Здорово!	Great! 122
зевать	to yawn 136
зевок	yawn 136
земля	ground 49
зеркало	mirror 40,74
знать	to know 36,61,73, 124,125,129,134
значить	to mean 157
зонтик	umbrella 115
зубная шётка	toothbrush 20
зубной врач	dentist 112
зубной пасты	toothpaste 22

И

игра	game 101,107,133
играть	to play 27,33,48,55,60, 67,78,80,90,91,97,101, 107,111,124
играть честно	to play fair 97
игрушка	toy 56,83,89
идея	idea 80
идёт дождь	It's raining 145,147
идти в плавание	to sail 97
идти (по)	to go 40,51,57,60,112, 114,118,119,136
идти на посадку	to land 92
идти в гости	to visit 38
идти спать	to go to bed 136,137
идти (по)	to suit 79
идти	to go outside 57,90

И

идти снег	to snow 147
идти (по)	to come 39,55, 67,110,152
идти	to follow 55
идти/ ходить	to walk 39,47, 58,78,89
извинить	to excuse 16
измерять	to measure 141
изучать	to study 71
имя	name 157
интереспо	interesting 126
искать (по)	to look for 25,36, 50,89,116
история	history 74, 75, 76
истратить	to spend 86

К

как	just 36
как	how 15,18,21,36, 72,77-79,122,144,(+)
как	like/ as 36,40
какой	kind of 132
камень	stone 50
камешек	pebble 54
карандаш	pencil 74,157
картина	picture 100
картофель	potato 29
карусель	merry-go-round 104
касса	cashier 89
кастрюля	pot 66
кататься на лодке	to go boating 98
кататься на роликовых досках	to skateboard 113
кататься	to skate 105
кататься на лыжах	to ski 117
кататься на водных лыжах	waterskiing 114
кататься на роликовых коньках	to roller skate 113
кататься на качелях	to swing 104
каток	rink 105
качели	swing 104

К

каша	cereal 30
кашель	cough 141, 142
кашлять	to cough 141
квадрат	square 101
кенгуру	kangaroo 103
кино	movies 110
класть	to put in 55
клумба	flower bed 68
книга	book 60,73,137
ковёр	rug 57
когда	when 20,61, (+)
когда	while 80
колено	knee 21,140
колено	lap 35
коллекция марка	stamp collection 108
коляска	carriage 40,44,48
комиксы	comic book 114
комната	room 43,44,51,57, 61,67,81,92
компьютер игра	computer game 101
компьютер	computer 60,69,91
Конечно!	Indeed! 129
конёк	skate 105
копать	to dig 68
корзина	wastebasket 77
кормить	to feed 32,61,102
коробка	box 46
косить	to mow 67
косточка	pit, seed 31
кошка	cat 46, 157
кран	faucet 21
красивый	pretty 79,102
красивый	beautiful 78,144
красный	red 103
крепко	tightly 104,157
кровать	bed 139
круг	circle 101, 105
кружиться	dizzy 140
крутить педали	to pedal 95
крутый	steep 118
крючок	hook 113
кто	who 13,29,36,125
кто	whose 122
кто-нибудь	anyone 76
кубик	block 38,42
кувшинка	water lily 103
куда	where 37,111

К

кукарекать	to crow 103
кукольный	puppet (adj) 112
кулка	doll 102
купить	to buy 67, 84-86
куртка	jacket 25,145
кусать	to bite 25,38,42
кусок	piece 30,69,107,135
кусок	puzzle piece 107
кухня	kitchen 44,57
кушать	to eat 29,57

Л

ласково	gently 42
лаять	to bark 103
левый	left (adj) 105
легушка	frog 103
лежать в постели	to stay in bed 138,142
лестница	stairs 41, 48
лето	summer 145
лечь	to lie down 116,138
лёгкий	easy 77, 107, 157
ливень	shower 146
лидер	leader 105
лист	leaf 68
лифт	elevator 85
лицо	face 19
ловить	to catch 94, 103
лодка	boat 97, 98
Ложись!	Lie down! 138
ложиться	to lean 46
ложка	spoon 31
локоть	elbow 29
лопата	shovel 115
лужа	puddle 146
лужайка	lawn 67
лучше	better 76,92, 125,142
лучше и лучше	better and better 80
лыжная палка	ski pole 117
лыжни	skis 117
лыжные ботики	ski boots 117
любить	to like, love 75,103
любить	to love 79,80,139

M

маг. деликатесов	delicatessen 83
магазин игрушек	toy store 83
мал	small 88
маленький	small 36
мальчик	boy 79,126
мама	mommy 39,65, 139,151
манера	way 80
масло	butter 59, 66
машина	car 99, 100
мебель	furniture 89
медленно	slowly 47,52
медуза	jelly fish 116
между	between 20
месить	to knead 66
места	room/ place 93
места	spot (place) 44
метро	subway 112
мечать	to dream 36 (wishing)
милный	kind 81
милый	cute 79
милый	sweet 79
минус	minus 152
минуту	moment 44
мишка	teddy bear 42
много	much 21,22,33,86
много	a lot 65,86,135
много	many 68
Мо-лод-цы!	Way to go! 106
может быть	perhaps 86,147
можно	may/can 30,67,76, 91,100,143
мокрый	wet 139, 146
молитва	prayer 138, 143
молния	lightening146
Молодец!	Well done! 80
молоко	milk 31,32,33,82
море	sea 115
море	ocean 114
морковь	carrot 30
мороженое	ice cream 133,135
мочь	(to be) able 102,108, 112,122,133
музыка	music 39,40,61,76
мука	flour 65
мусор	garbage 61, 68
мыло	soap 22

M

мыть (по)	to wash 19,20, 23,64,69
мышь	mouse 37
мягий	soft 118
мясо	meat 31, 82
мяч	ball 38,42,94,106

Н

на улицу	outside 56,90,93
наблюдать(по)	to observe 116
наверх	upstairs 51,57
нагрузить	to load 108
надеть	to put on, wear 25,26, 42,51,96,137
надеяться	to hope 127
надо	to have to 137
надо	must 71, 43
надувной матрас	air mattress 115
надуть	to blow up 105
наживка	bait 113
найти	to find 56
накрыть	to set (table) 63
налево	left (adv) 49, 95
налить	to fill 21,32
налить	to pour 32
нападать	to charge 103
направо	right (adv) 49, 95
напугать	to frighten 34
настольная игра	board game 96
настроение	mood 52
насыпать	to pour 65
наука	science 72
начать	to begin 71,76,147
начертить	to draw 78
начинать	to start 70,73,76,147
нашуники	headset 61
не спить	awake 139
не торопиться	to take one's time 58
небо	sky 115, 146
небольшой	a little 74
невероятно	unbelievable 126
нельзя	must not 59,130
немедленно	immediately 55

Н

немного	a little 31,41,86
неправа	wrong 130
нервничай	nervous 53
несколько	some 153
несколько	few, several 153
нести (от)(при)	to carry 50,103
неудачный	bad 86
нефтевоз	oil truck 109
нефть	oil 109
нижнее бельё	underpants 25
новый	new 15, 26,41,67, 85,98,113
нога	foot 42,85,105,142
ноготь	nail (finger) 25
нож	knife 31,49
ножницы	scissors 72
нос	nose 40, 54
носок	sock 138
нравиться (по)	to like 32,37,41,80, 88,89,103,109
Ну-ка!	Come on! 35
нужно	to have to 25,67,72,75, 84,102,138,142,157(+)
нужно	to need 23,74,76,105(+)
нужно	must/ should 47,50,87

О

оба	both 48, 93
обед	lunch 33,49,65
обедать	to lunch 28
обжечься	to burn oneself 48
облачен	cloudy 145
обляко	cloud 144
обнимать	to hug 15
обовной магазин	shoe store 84
обращать	to pay attention 46,48
обрезать	to prune 68
обувь	shoe 137
обязательно	necessary 128
огород	vegetable garden 68
одежда	clothes 66,67,85,137,138
озеро	lake 99,114
окно	window 46,107
опаздывать	to be late 62
опасно	dangerous 69, 118

О

Опасно!	Danger! 130
опухший	swollen 141
опять	again 96, 145
оставить	to leave 46
Остановись!	Stop! 43
остановиться	to stop 71
остаться	to stay 43,44,85, 111,117,142
осторожно	(Be) careful 31,32, 48,93,101,122
Осторожно!	Look out! 68,130
острый	sharp 49
отверстие	opening 85
отвечать	responsible 58
отдохнуть	to rest 107,119,124,141
отец	father 36
открытка	card 133
открыть	to open 46,54
открыть	to turn on faucet 21
отойти на шаг	to step back 47
отправляться	to start 110
отправляться	All aboard! 97,108
Отпусти!	Let go! 35
отталкивать	to push off 98,105
очень	very 15,95,126,127
очень	a lot 43
очередь	turn 45,61,94,96,115
очистить	to sand 69
очки от солнце	sunglasses 117

П

пазл	puzzle 107
падать	to fall 147
палатка	tent 99
палец	finger 49,142,151
пальто	coat 26, 87, 88
папа	daddy 25,42,65(+)
парк	park 133
пахнуть	to smell 22,31
педаль	pedal 94
первый	first 56
перебегать	to run (across) 48
перед	before 20,48,67,137
передать	to pass 31,106

П

передходить	to cross 49
перекусить	to snack 29
переночевать	to sleep over 143
переодеться	to change clothes 26
перестать	to stop 45,54,59,60, 147,159
перечатка	glove 25
период жары	heat wave 145
перо	feather 103
песня	song 40
песочница	sandbox 93
петух	rooster 103
петь	to sing 35, 78
печенье	cookie 30,65,75,151
печь	to bake 65,66,75
пижама	pajama 42,137
пикник	picnic 133
пила	saw 114
пилот	pilot 92
писать	to write 47,78,157
пить (вы)	to drink 31,118
пища	pizza 29
плавить	to swim 78,93,114,115
плакатный картон	poster board 72
плакать	to cry 38, 42
пластинки	brace (teeth) 113
плащ	cape 103
плескаться	to splash 38
плитка	stove 99
плотенце	towel 22, 115
плохо(й)	bad 53, 142
плошадка	playground 62,90,103,111
пляж	beach 114, 133
по магазинам	shopping 67, 89
по-английски	English 18
победить	to win 122
побриться	to shave 23
побродить по магазинам	window shopping 89
повернуться	to turn around 37
повестить	to hang 22,138
погладить ласково	to pet 43
погремушка	rattle 35
подарок	present 67,132,133,135
подбрать	to pick up 47,138
подгузник	diaper 24
поделить	to divide 135

П

поддерживать	to keep 95
подключить	to hook up 69
подметать	to sweep 65, 69
поднять	to raise 35
поднять	to lift 105
подняться	to climb up 41
подогнать	adjusted 113,117
пододвинуть	to move closer 63
подойти на шаг	to step forward 47
подстилка	blanket 115,116
Поедем!	Let's go! 111,114
пожалуйста	please 37,49,50
Пожар!	Fire! 105
пожарник	fireman 134
пожарное отделение	fire department 105
позаботиться	to take care 42
позвонить	to ring 39
поздно	late 61,116,137,149,150
познакомиться	to meet 18
поиск	search 102
Пойдём!	Let's go! 111,114
пойти на рыбалку	to go fishing 113,114
пойти домой	to go home 119
показать	to show 36,39,51,55,(+)
поключиться к интернету	to go on-line 75
покрасить	to dye 113
пол	floor 47, 65
поле	field 91
поливать	to water 68
полно	filled 64
полный	full 32
положить	to put 22,46,47,64, 68,69,99,102,107
пользоваться	to use 31
Помедленнее!	Slow down! 98
Помоги!	Help! 105
помочь	to help 16,49,56,63-69, 73,76,85,105,122
понимать	to understand 54,73
попасть	to miss 94
попробовать	to taste 30
пора	time 25,70
пора вернуть	to be due 60

П

порвать	to tear 101	пробовать(по)	to try 31,58,95
порт	port 97	проверить	to check 99
поручная горка	slide 104	провести	to have a good time
после	after 14,20,33,66,111	время	16
послушный	naughty 53	программа	program 60
посмотреть	to look at 37,39,48,52,	прогуляться	to stroll 40
	69,87,114,157	проект	project 72
поставить	to set 66	проиграть	to lose 97,106
поставить	to pitch (tent) 99	прокататься на	to take a car ride 113
поставить	to put 47,56,58,94	машине	
пострисься	to get a haircut 23	пролить	to spill 33
посуда	dishes 64	прополоть сад	to weed 68
потереть	to rub 37,54	пропустить	to skip (omit) 76
потерять	to lose 76	просторен	loose 88
потеть	to sweat 145	простудиться	to catch cold 116
потолкнуть	to push 99	прохладно	cool 145
потом	then 57	прочистить	to floss 20
потом	later 23	Прочь!	Get out! 43
потому что	because 38,49	прыгать	to jump 47,93,104
Поторопись!	Hurry! 43	прямо	right (adv) 99
поточить	to sharpen 105	прямо	straight 35,52,95
потушить	to turn out the light 57	прямо-	rectangle 101
похоже	looks like 147	угольник	
поцеловать	to kiss 16	прятять	to hide 91,103
почему нет	why not 64	птица	bird 100, 116
почему	why 33,38,124,130,139	пудинг	pudding 32
почистить	to brush 20	пузо	tummy 79
почта	post office 84	пузырь	bubble 93
правда	true 125,129	пусть	to have (allow) 124
правильно	right (fair) 128	пылесос	vacuum cleaner 65
правильно	correct/ly 29,125	пылесосить(про)	to vacuum 65,69
правый	right 24, 105	пыль	dust 65
прежде	before 22, 35	пытаться (по)	to try/ test 55,80,131
привести	to bring 15	пьеса	play 112
приглашать	to invite 60,133		
прийти	to come 50,57,61,91	Р	
приклеить	to paste 100,101		
примерять	to try on 87	работа по дому	chore 111
принимать	to take 23,143	работа	work 25,71,77
принять	to take (bath) 21,23	работать	to work 65,71,74,77
принести	to get/ bring 42,49,55,115	равновесие	balance 95
пристегнуть	to fasten 60,92	рад	glad 14,18,71,122
причесать	to comb 26, 102	радостно	sad 122
приятный	nice 37,77	радуга	rainbow 147
		разбить	to break 42

Р

разбрызгиватель	sprinkler 68
разбудить	to awaken 140
разговорчивый	talkative 35
разделить на	divided by 152
размер	size 87
разобрать	to sort 108
разписать	to print 102
разрешено	allowed, may 56,90
разрыхлитель	baking powder 66
раковина	sink 20,64
ракушки	seashells 116
рано	early 61,137,139,149
раскатать	to roll 101
раскачивать	to push 104
раскрасить	to color 100
распилить	to saw 69
рассказ	story 37,66,137
расстелить	to spread 115
расходы	allowance 67
расчёска	comb 26
рвать	to pick 93
ребёнок	baby 40, 51
резать (по) (вы)	to cut 32,49,100,135
резаться	to teethe 139
ремень безопас ности	seat belt 60, 92
ресторан	restaurant 133
рисовать (на)	to paint 75,100
рисовать	to draw 101
рот	mouth 32,37,40,54
рубашка	shirt 25,50,51,138
рука	hand 19,24,31,41,42, 48,54,65,81,106,128
рука	arm 36,41,142
рукав	sleeve 24,41
руль	handlebars 95
ручка	handle 48
рыба	fish 72,114
рычать	to growl 103

С

сад	garden 68,74,112
салфетка	napkin 64
самолёт	airplane 92

С

сандвич	sandwich 30
сахар	sugar 66
сверкать	to sparkle 147
свет	light 22,48,56,139
светить	to shine 145
светый	light (adj)146
свечка	candle 134
свитер	sweater 88,145
сгрести	to rake 68
сгрести	to shovel 67
сдаваться	to give up 80,123
сделать	to do / make 16,30, 37, 45,49,50,51,55, 58,59,74,76,80,102, 122,128
сделать потише	to lower(volume) 59
себя	yourself 30,53,60
сегодня	today 28,71,146
сейчас	now 43,45,73,119
семя	seed 68
серый	grey 146
сестра	sister 36,50,73,116,151
сесть	to sit down 29,35,41,93
сесть	to get in 113
сжать	to squeeze 31
сидеть	to sit 35,93,103
сильный	strong 79,91
сильный	a lot 119
синий	blue 25, 96
сирена	siren 105
сказать	to say 131
сказать (раз)	to tell 20,50,58, 73,137
скакалка	jump rope 104
скачать	to miss 15
складывать	to fold 66
скобка	staple 72
сколько	how many/ how much 21,86,87,95,118,152
сколько времени	how long 92,98,148

С

скользкий	slippery 22
скорого	later 16
скотч	scotch tape 72
сладкий	sweet 32
слегка	gently 104
следить	to keep an eye on 94
следовать	to follow 105
слишить	to hear 34,38,62
слишком	too much 21,32,61,68, 69,86,88,95,107(+)
слово	word 157
сложить	to fold 22, 101
сломать	to break 42
сломаться	to break down 99
случиться	to happen 58,127
слушать (по)	to listen 35,52,113
смелый	brave 79
смешной	funny 126
смеяться	to laugh 130
смотреть (по)	to look at 35,37,39, 48,52,107,145
смотреть (по)	to watch 41,59,68, 69,114,116,117,137
Смывайся!	Scram! 103
снаряжение	equipment 117
снег	snow 145,147
снеговик	snowman 147
снежинка	snowflake 147
сновидение	dream 143
снять	to take off 62, 137
собака	dog 42,61,92,103,127
собрать	to pick up 101
сок	juice 33
солёный	salty 32
солнечно	sunny 144
солнце	sun 100,115
соль	salt 31
сорняк	weed 68
сортировать	to sort 66
соус	sauce 32
спальный мешок	sleeping bag 99
спасательная шлюпка	life boat 98
Спасибо	Thanks 15,17,135
Спасите !	Help! 122
спаться	to sleep 51,138,140,142
спача	change 88

С

спектакль	show 112
спешить	to hurry 44,47
Спи спокойно!	Sleep well! 143
список	list 82
спокойный	calm/ quiet 107,115
спросить	to ask 50,57,91,127
спусать	to lower (boat) 98
спустить	to empty 22
спустить	to flush 20
спустить	to slide down 104
ссориться	to quarrel 58
стакан	glass 32
становиться	to get, become 80, 138,145
стараться(по)	to try 76,95
стеклярнный шарик	marble (toy) 104
стена	wall 47,160
степлер	stapler 72
стирать (вы)	to wash 64,138
стирать (по)	to launder 64
стирка	laundry 22
стоить	to cost 108
стол	table 28,29,33,47, 63,64,108
стоять лагерем	to camp 98, 99
стрелять	to shoot 104
строить (по)	to build 69,114,116
стул	chair 41,63,115
сумка	pouch/ bag 89,103
сунуть (про)	to put into 42,85
супермаркет	supermarket 84
считать	to count 88,134,152
сыграть	to play 40, 108
сюда (от)	here 39.43,55,107

Т

так	so 16,31,57,95
так много	so much 22,33,68
так много	so long 123
там	over there 87,89
там	there 44,89,96
тарелка	plate 33
твёрдный	hard 118
телевизор	television 59

T

T

тележка для покупок	shopping cart 85	убирать	to put back 67
телефон	telephone 80	убирать	to clear 64
темнота	dark 56	убрать	to clean 64,66,67,81
темный	dark 146	угадать	to guess 103
температура	temperature 141	ударить	to hit 42
температура	fever 140	ударить	to swing (bat) 94
тень	shade 115	ударять	to bump 55
теперь	now 135,160	ударять	to kick 38,42,106
тепло	warm 118,119,145	удачная	good buy 86
терпение	patience 53	покупка	
тесто	dough 66	удочка	fishing rod 113
тихо	quietly 43,80	ужасный	awful 126, 146
тише	softly 53	ужин	dinner 28,29
Тише!	(Be) quiet! 43,138	уйти	to come away 45
тоже	too (also) 30,91,126,131	узок	tight 88
только что + verb	to have just 70,115	улица	street 48,95,146
только	just 127	уложить	to put to bed 137
только	only 150	улыбка	smile 37
только что	just 70	улыбнуться	to smile 36
тонуть	to sink 97	уметь	to know how 157
топливо	fuel 92	универмаг	department store 83
торговый центр	mall 84,110	управлчть	to drive (a boat) 98
тормозить	to brake 96	упрямый	stubborn 54
торт	cake 65,133,135	урок	lesson 72,76,77
треугольник	triangle 101	уронить	to drop 49
трогать	to touch 42,47,55,106	успалый	tired 118,136
тротуар	sidewalk 56, 69	успокоить	to calm oneself 53,127
трудный	hard/ difficult 72,77,107	установить	to set up 99
тряпка	dust cloth 65	устроить	to have (arrange) 133
туалет	bathroom 19	утро	morning 14,73,149
туда	there 45,47,119	ухо	ear 19, 40
туда	over there 47	уходить	to go away 44,46
туман	fog 146	уходить	to leave 94
туфлет	toilet 19,20	учиться	to study 75
туфля	shoe 24,42,47,58,146		
тяжёлый	heavy 138		

У

Ф

		форм	form 118
		фотографир-	to take (photo) 37
у + pronoun + есть	to have 89,98,100,113,	овать	
	117,120,133,141,151	фугрон	camper 98
у +	house 143	футбол	soccer 106,114
убаюкать	to rock asleep 52	футболка	t-shirt 26

Х

хватать	to grab 50	
хить	to live 18	
хлеб	bread 32, 82	
хлопать	to clap 40	
хозяйственная сумка	shopping bag 89	
холодильник	refrigerator 58	
холодный	cold 21,116,118	
хорошо	good 16,23,31,53, 73,79,80,127,142,151	
хорошо	right (correct) 65, 121	
хорошо	all right 121	
хорошо	nice 26,85,118	
хорошо	well 15,78,142(+)	
хотеть сказать	to mean 131	
хотеть	to want 23,25,29,30,41, 44,45,51,52,55,62,65, 69,85 (+)	
хотеть	to like/ want 22,28,38, 44,58,67,101,114,(+)	
хотеть	to wish 123	
хотеться	to feel like 27,73	
хочется пить	thirsty 28	
хочешь не хочешь	whether 112	

Ц

царапина	scratch 140
цвет	color 75,100, 165
цветный карандаш	crayon 55,76,100
цветок	flower 93

Ч

чай	tea 42
часы	clock 66
чашка	cup 42
Человек за бортом!	Man over board! 97
чердак	attic 114
через	through 24, 54, 85
честно	fairly 97
чистый	clean 21
читать (по)(про)	to read 66,73,75,114,137
чихать	to sneeze 141
что	what 15,25,28,34 (+)
что-нибудь	something 28,67,77,85, 86,118,142

Ч

чтобы	so 57,68
чувствовать	to feel 15,142

Ш

шахматы	chess 96
шашки	checkers 96
швабра	mop 49
шея	neck 20
шить	to sew 65
шкаф	cabinet 66
школа	school 71
шлем	helmet 96
шляпа	hat 88
шоколадный	chocolate 135
шпинат	spinach 32
штаны	pants 41
шум	noise 34
шутить	to joke 127
щётка	brush 26

Э

эскалатр	escalator 85

Ю

юбка	skirt 65

Я

язык	tongue 103,141
яйцо	egg 66
ясный	clear 115,127

(+) indicates many additional uses throughout the text.

Also by *Therese Slevin Pirz*

Kids Stuff Spanish
  Kids Stuff Inglés
    Kids Stuff Italian
      Kids Stuff German
        Kids Stuff French
          Kids Stuff Russian
            Kids Stuff Angliiski

ABC's of SAT's:
How One Student Scored 800 on the Verbal SAT
(An annotated reading list for children)

Coloring in .....(foreign language) Series: (Coloring books for children)
Coloring in Inglés
Coloring in Angliiski (English)